NOT BY ACCIDENT

NOT BY
ACCIDENT

recontructing a careless life

SAMANTHA DUNN

SHE WRITES PRESS

Published 2015
Printed in the United States of America
ISBN: 978-1-63152-832-3
Library of Congress Control Number: 2015937499

For information, address:
She Writes Press
1563 Solano Ave #546
Berkeley, CA 94707

She Writes Press is a division of SparkPoint Studio, LLC.

ALSO BY SAMANTHA DUNN:

Failing Paris

Faith in Carlos Gomez

Women on the Edge: Writing from Los Angeles (editor)

FOREWORD

After St. Augustine's *Confessions* and before the current wave of memoirs, Samantha Dunn wrote *Not By Accident*. It was widely hailed when it was published, and now its return is cause for another celebration.

Quite simply, *Not by Accident* is a classic in the genre—and book categories aside, it is simply a fine piece of writing that stands alone. In this memoir, a horseback-riding incident propels our heroine on an inward and outward journey that results in, yes, a return to the saddle of the horse that inadvertently almost killed her.

But how she started over and hit the trail again is a rich and multilayered story filled with beauty, anguish, and great humor—plus there's a bonus track in the form of lyrics from Ratt. More rocking yet, Michelangelo checks in for an important visit, along with various citizens of LA's healing community, including doctors who practice medicine Western-style, and yoga devotees whose practice is anything but. And through it all is Sam's beloved thoroughbred Harley, waiting to reconnect with his partner when she—and he—is ready.

The accident—but was it really? For the answer, you must read this book!—happens like this: One day, life-long equestrienne Sam takes Harley out for a ride. They follow a trail that others are praising for its new wildflower blooms and waterfall at its end, and soon they reach a flowing creek—unusual in these California drylands and not something Harley—skittish, as are all thoroughbreds—is accustomed to.

He is reluctant to cross it. Sam dismounts and coaxes him into the water, smoothing his coat, "which," she writes, "seems like the skin of an eel, then a mink, oiled and slick." Realizing she is wearing new paddock boots, she skips across the water, not wanting to get them wet. The unfamiliar noise roils Harley; he rears up and Sam is flung and knocked over, stunned and watching as the 2,100-pound horse comes down on her left shin, nearly slicing off the leg with his hoof. Bleeding profusely and unable to move, she lies for a time in paralysis, flooded by memories and fears, wondering if this is the end, right here in the wilderness with emergency services and water and tourniquets just moments away. Trees, birds, and flowers stand out in bas-relief, yet nature's song makes no difference. As Sam writes so eloquently in her book, "The loudest sound is my own breath. Everything is perfectly ordered, the quick rise and fall of my chest. The ground, the chlorophyll sweetness of grass, the squawk of a scrub jay, the rush of breeze in the oaks overhead. People have died to these sounds for thousands of years."

But somewhere inside these seemingly last moments, her grandmother—dead for a decade—pays her a visit. "What the hell's the matter with you?" the voice harangues. "You're not dead yet. You can still scream." And scream Sam does—a person who never wanted to ask for help now calling for it in a place where, quite possibly, no one is listening.

To her surprise, someone is listening—and, in fact, since this is California, and Los Angeles, and Malibu at that, that someone is a famous actor, Edward Albert, Jr., who ambles in through the chapparal, just like in the movies. He happens to live nearby, and was working his horses with a friend when he heard the cry. He administers first aid and calls paramedics, who chopper in, and then Sam is whisked away to the hospital. There, a series of several surgeries begins, followed by months of pain and the unraveling of her life and all of the attendant questions. As Edward Albert tells her months later, "I remember seeing you in the dirt, and the look in your eye. I said to myself, this has the reek of karma all over it. It was literally a breaking point. You could go one way or the other."

As she always has in her life, Sam took the road less travelled—and then wrote about it so we could all make sense of our own painful and marvelous journeys into parts unknown. I met Sam shortly after *Not by Accident* was first published. I was working on my book *Mustang: The Saga of the Wild Horse in the American West*, and some of our mutual friends in the literary community of Los Angeles suggested that I read her book, not just because it was about horses, or rather that a horse was part of the story, but because one of its concerns was how fraught is our relationship with them. Although my book was about wild horses and Sam's had to do with a domestic horse, both works examined the role of the horse in our lives, in all its splendor and tragedy, and its never-ending ability to help us escape the shackles of daily life and burdens.

Years into my book, I became fearful of finishing. I had become so close with one of the horses in it that I believed she had survived a massacre to serve as my guide through the story of her kind. Once I pressed the send button, her raison d être would be wiped out and she would perish. Grandiose perhaps, but such was my fear at the time. On the other hand, what if something happened to me during the course of writing—and I couldn't finish the story? It was part of my life's work; who would complete it if I could not? The only writer who could finish the task at hand was Samantha Dunn. The task was not to cook up the second half of my sentences but to recount the majesty and tragedy of the horse, in this case through the prism of our national life and yearnings. So well had Sam understood how the very being of the horse is woven into our narratives and selves; how in awe I was of her writing as she described the moment that she rides Harley again, for the first time, after the accident:

Harley stands quietly, flicks his ears as if waiting for
directions. What now, boss? *My leg immediately*
starts to throb from the pressure of hanging but I
ignore it for now. My hands run over his shoulders,
I inhale the smell of him, the scent of oil and dried
sweat, a single green stalk of alfalfa tangled in his
mane. I grab a handful, the wiry black strands.
How like suture thread; I never noticed that before.

I never noticed that before either, not that I had cause to, but how right, I thought when I read that, a mane like suture thread! How necessary, how always. Yet I never asked Sam if she would finish my book should the occasion arise, only told her years later, too embarrassed to admit to such a need at the time, certainly not ready to call out for help.

"Do you think I'll ever dance again?" Sam asks her doctor after one of his early and extremely dire pronouncements about the state of her leg. It wasn't that she was a person who danced, but now she was kind of wondering. How could she do that, after all, with one leg? But really, it wasn't just the prospect of being one-legged, it was something well beyond that. People who have near-death experiences, who come face-to-face with that well-known white light and then return, often report that they regret not having used the body in which they dwell; in fact they feel they have disappointed the shelter that can provide them with so much pleasure. They vow to begin anew, letting the senses take them where they may, and they advise us to join them. Sam did in fact dance again, or for the first time, and then wrote about that too, in another fantastic memoir called *Faith in Carlos Gomez: A Memoir of Salsa, Sex, and Salvation.* It will make you want to swing your hips, baby, but that's a subject for another discussion.

For now, I'll conclude by saying that the memoir genre is lucky to have Sam—and so are we. And with this new edition of *Not by Accident*, there can be no mistake and no forgetting: Samantha Dunn is a modern master—regardless of what shelf this book appears on.

DEANNE STILLMAN

I.

Thoroughbreds are by definition
nervous horses.

It begins with a jerk and click, as if a projector is being turned on in the middle of a film. A winding canyon trail is in front of me. Autumn leaves mottle the late afternoon light that filters down. I ease the leather of well-oiled reins between my fingers.

Today I'd arrived a little later than usual, was not up for the concentration it takes to work in the ring. Was on the phone all day, forgot to pay the electric bill. Two realtors showed up, unexpected. The landlord is going to sell the house, a thirty day notice, thanks a lot. I was impatient to just get out in the hills where the mustard weeds are still blooming, a sea of yellow that comes up to my horse's belly. This trail is supposed to lead up to a waterfall. Everybody at the stable comes back with reports of its beauty, but for some reason my horse and I have never been up there. Not that far, maybe five miles round trip. The usual route at the beginning, a very narrow track along the edge of an arroyo that rises steeply to the top of a ridge. I tilt forward in the saddle as we climb, taking my weight off his back. The sun and the incline soon make him sweat, darkening his bay coat.

We come to the turn for the waterfall, going down into the canyon. The trees grow taller, the brush more dense. The path twists, it's impossible to see what lies around the next bend.

All at once we're in front of a narrow creek, unexpected in the dryness of Southern California. My horse freezes as if we have come upon a giant anaconda rather than the simple flow of water this is. He shakes his head, every muscle taut as a metal spring, and chews on his bit, foam from his mouth flying with every toss of his head. This is his way of saying, You didn't warn me about this! Why didn't you warn me about this?

I ignore him. Thoroughbreds are by definition nervous horses; mine is no exception. I can feel his back round, the shift of his weight onto his haunches. He wants to jump this obstacle and take off, I just want to make it to the top of the trail before dusk.

I slip my feet from the stirrups and dismount. It will be faster to guide him through this than negotiate a settlement. "C'mon Harley," I say as I begin to lead him to the creek, "don't be a sissy."

His head descends toward the creek to sniff the water, creating an arch with his neck. His large brown eyes, the color of malt balls, can't gauge the depth of the water.

"Relax sweetie," I tell him, reaching far up above my head to smooth my hand over his coat. It first seems like the skin of an eel, then a mink, oiled and slick. I realize that I'm wearing my new paddock boots. I don't want to get them wet, so as I lead Harley I skip over the water.

It is small motion, really.

All at once I have a sense of being flung. Then the surprise as the bony force of Harley's knee suddenly pushes into my back. A kind of nausea. My 1,200-pound horse has reared back. He is now jumping forward. And he is landing on top of me.

Dirt in my mouth as I'm pushed to the ground. The odd beauty of the angle formed by my arm as it pops out of my shoulder. I feel no pain right now, aware only of how mammoth my horse appears as he stands over me, blocking all sun. He snorts, not able to see me under him but knowing by scent I'm there. His muscles quiver. His sweat drips onto my face; perhaps it is my own.

"Harley, easy boy, easy."

But his body pulls away and I see the flash of the steel-shod hoof as it strikes downward. I hear the crack of something, loud as gunfire, and look to see my left leg snapped apart like dry kindling.

His hind hoof has just come through the middle of my left shin, cutting like a dull shovel straight through the bones, the muscles, ligaments and veins. Only a hinge of calf muscle and sinew remain.

■ ■ ■

It can't be as bad as it looks, I think. It really can't be this bad.

■ ■ ■

I try to stand, or at least I have the intention. Maybe I pass out. Grains of dirt roll against the enamel of my teeth. I lick my lips.

I have to remove my lace-up paddock boot. I have to, I have to, I have to. Last month when I fell down the flight of stairs and badly sprained this same ankle, the area ballooned, making the process of removing my shoe complicated. And then what about that young horse. Slammed me against a gate, smashed my right side, and my right foot swelled. Had to wear it for a few hours and that hurt like hell. That fallen horse, what was his name? Romeo. His hoof struck my toe as he struggled to his feet. What was wrong with Romeo? I couldn't bother with the boot then. When I finally got around to taking it off, there was so much swelling the laces had to be cut to spread the leather wide enough.

I reach to untie the laces. The dead weight of my own foot feels like meat. With each beat of my heart, blood flows out of my body into the ground like a garden hose left running on the lawn.

I lay back in the dirt, exhausted, boot still on. Forget it. My horse grazes as if he has never eaten, quickly tearing the grass with his teeth. His reins drag across the ground as he mows from clump to clump. What if he steps through his reins, becomes tangled and breaks a leg? He can't break a leg. They shoot horses with broken legs.

■ ■ ■

The loudest sound is my own breath. Everything is perfectly

ordered, the quick rise and fall of my chest. The ground, the chlorophyll sweetness of grass, the squawk of a scrub jay, the rush of breeze in the oaks overhead. People have died to these sounds for thousands of years.

But people can't die this way today.

I can't die this way today.

■ ■ ■

I am picturing the time I was in my living room with my sprained foot propped up, talking to my friend Lucia. But as I think of her she changes, her African skin becomes a leopard, her black almond eyes turn orange and watch me. I am lamenting a string of bad luck that has seemed to come my way these months, the tumble down the stairs, a fall from Harley in which I sprain my back, crack my tailbone. She is not sympathetic.

"God touches us with a feather to get our attention," she growls at me. "Then if we don't listen, he starts throwing bricks."

The same breeze, the same grass. I cannot say if a moment or an hour has passed since the last time I saw the light coming through the oaks. My blood pools around me. Harley stops grazing and puts his nose to my face. The inside of his nostrils are plush as old velvet.

He takes a step nearer to me, snorts loudly, sniffing the overripe scent that is the smell of blood escaped. I push his head away, afraid of him for the first time in my life. Hooves of a beast. At the core we are both animals, propelled by fear and basic impulses.

"Get, get!" I shrill at him, "Don't step on me again! Please, damn it, just get away!"

Then a voice starts yelling in my ear with a tone and pitch exactly like that of my grandmother, says, *What the hell's the matter with you?* My grandmother is dead 10 years. The voice is coming from the inside of my head but sounds as if she's standing right in back of me. *You're not dead yet. You can still scream. Sam, scream. For chrissake, scream.*

I prop myself up on the uninjured arm. I take a deep

breath. I open my mouth.

I have never heard my own voice truly scream. It is ugly, not unlike the sound a rabbit makes when caught by a pack of coyotes. I raise goosebumps on my own skin.

A rustling from up the trail. Coyotes, damn them, or could it be deer? A dog? No, the sound in the dirt in a one-two-one-two rhythm. Feet.

A blond man running reaches me. But he steps back, afraid to touch me. By the look on his face it seems he is going to throw up.

"I'm fine," I say, although the way he recoils means the situation is even worse than it looks to me. "Please, just get my horse. He's going to step through those reins."

"Right," he says. "Right. I'm sorry. You stay there."

"Right," I answer. Where, exactly, would I be going with half a leg?

Probably he meant to say that help is on its way. It arrives seconds later. Another man, this one with dark hair, runs through the dry brush and stands over me. He is an actor whose face I recognize, a disorienting fact that makes me consider perhaps I am already dead and have been sent to a special Purgatory for Los Angelenos.

"Can you hear me? Can you hold on?" I think that's what he says. I know for sure that he kneels beside me without hesitation. I remember him in a role from a movie with Goldie Hawn I had seen on cable. Maybe I truly am dead. Maybe this is St. Peter revealing himself as an actor with a good tan and even smile. His voice is deep and does not betray any sense of panic. He has on a choker with a tooth or claw in the center. I have a sudden desire to fluff my hair and wipe the dirt from my face.

"I've had a little accident," I tell him.

"I can see." He asks me if I can move my arms, if my head is hurt.

"My leg is kind of messed up," I tell him. "And I think I might be dead."

"You're very much alive, and you're going to stay that

way," he says. "We're going to get some help. What's your name sweetheart?"

"Sam," I say. I want to be polite about this but politeness takes time. "I know you're an actor, can you please tell me your name? I'm sorry, I feel like I should know it—"

"Edward Albert," he says, "and please, don't—"

"Green Acres? You're not that old—"

"That's my dad. I've been in a few movies, but don't worry about that."

Of course I'm not dead because I can still feel embarrassed. The idea is comforting. "I'm sorry, I should have—"

"Please, you've got a few other things going on right now." His voice resonates like an iron bell. "Are you hurt anywhere else?"

"My shoulder."

"Let's see," he says, looking me over. He touches my shoulder. "I'm trying to remember anything useful from the times I've played a doctor."

"I feel better already."

"Ssh," you don't have to talk, just relax," he says.

"But I need to talk," I say.

He tells me that they'd been coming from their barn, he and Dave, the blond man, they'd been working the horses. They heard a screech. He says he was going to ignore it, he thought it was the cry of a bird, sometimes the red tail hawks make this kind of sound, but his daughter said No Dad, I think it's someone yelling for help.

I hear Edward tell someone, it must be Mr. I-Think-I'm-Going-to-Throw-Up, We probably can't get a signal here on your cell phone. Can we? No? Run back and call 911. Hurry. Lead the horse back to the house and tell Ty to call.

What follows must include a call to paramedics, questions about whom to call in case of emergency. I remember a telephone number, but I can't recall what it's to.

"Is Harley OK? Do you think he'll be all right?" I need to know.

"He's great. He's sorry about the accident," I think Edward says.

"That's OK," I say, "he didn't mean to."

"He didn't mean to," Edward echoes.

He smoothes my hair back from my forehead in a rhythmic motion. I keep trying to raise my head to look down to where my leg lies, but the pressure of his palm against my forehead becomes more insistent and I realize he's keeping me from lifting my head up and seeing what's going on. I am aware of how green his eyes are but I cannot see his hands. There is no tourniquet.

He says, "I'd carry you, but I'm afraid—" He does not complete his sentence, but I know what he cannot tell me. Since muscle and skin are the only materials keeping my leg from being completely severed, the dead weight would likely tear the rest of the leg off if he tried to lift me.

And then, what to do with all this blood? I don't know how he stays with me here in the dirt. Help takes a while; shadows slant more sharply through the oaks, that crystal time of day just before dusk when the light draws the world in perfect relief. The breeze seems colder by degree.

Sometime later I hear a young woman's voice shouting down the trail, "Dad! The paramedics can't find you!"

The paramedics can't find us, and that breeze is getting so cold. I want to move my arm to get comfortable, but no such angle exists that will bring comfort.

"Well, go get them," Edward shouts back, the first time I hear the tinny ring of tension in his voice. But then he turns to me, smiles. "That's my daughter, Ty." He tells me she was born into his arms, and his was the first face she saw. This explains him. Here is a man who has seen a woman bleed before.

He tells me many things about his life, he asks me about mine. The way two people talk when one is keeping the other from bleeding to death is its own category of conversation.

"Do you think I'll ever dance again?" I ask him, out of nowhere. I don't even know how to dance. But now I'm thinking it's something I would want to do if I could. "Why haven't I been dancing all my life? Doesn't it seem dumb that I don't rumba? The electric slide?"

"You'll dance," he says.

I shut my eyes and his voice surrounds me just as a blanket would. It talks to me about Ireland, and the exact color of heather. The voice, which seems to be the only voice, ever, asks me, Have you ever been there?

No.

You must go.

Now?

No, when you're better. Surely your family is originally from Ireland, surely with auburn hair and freckles.

Yes.

The Irish are fine horsemen.

As fine as the Spanish.

My mother was from Mexico.

Fine horsemen they are, too.

The paramedics materialize out of the dry brush. The looks on their faces provide no reassurance; I realize that somewhere I held the notion they would tell me the situation wasn't that dire, that I only have a broken leg. Many people break their leg. It happens every day. I was even afraid of inconveniencing them. "We came all the way out here for this, lady?" they'd say.

Instead they talk on walkie-talkies, they've seen this kind of thing before in the canyons but this is a bad one, horses are dangerous animals, why would anyone want to get on a horse? Do you have insurance? Yes? What kind? Do you happen to remember your social security number? No, but I can remember the first phone number we had when I was a child, 435-4351, that doesn't help, does it?

But I have insurance, so there will be a medi-vac helicopter to take me to UCLA's trauma center. They will have to cut away the rest of my breeches, do I mind? They're pretty well torn, I say, they're old anyway. But my boots are still good.

Did I mention to you guys that I didn't want to get them wet? I have on black cotton underwear with stretchy lace, my mother would be proud. The paramedic with a mustache asks, Where can the helicopter land up here? Is there level ground within a mile? You can't possibly be asking me that question. No one seems to know.

I think they also ask if I have pain anywhere else, or maybe one of them touches the arm that is pulled out of the socket. Somehow it ends up that one of them pulls my arm straight, and then moves it slightly. The joint pops back into place, my body like the box of doll parts I had as a child, a collection of Barbie legs, a head, arms, torsos of varying sizes.

I think I must cry out during that, because suddenly again I am looking up through those leaves.

"Can't you give her something?" Edward's voice again. He holds my hand. "Valium, anything?"

They're sorry but no, not until x-rays. There could be head injury, there could be who knows what.

Edward keeps holding my hand. "Squeeze when it hurts," he says.

"But your fingers are turning purple."

He tells me not to worry, that worry implies the absence of faith. Here, in this dirt, is exactly where I need to be. The Chumash tribe considered this very ground sacred, he says. He knows some Chumash, they still believe it. "Your life will change because of this," he tells me, "in ways you can't imagine now."

I try to focus on his eyes, they seem farther away, and I have a peculiar sensation of looking up through a hole that is getting deeper and more narrow. A drain. If I were to feel water fill my lungs at this moment it would not be a surprise.

"It's here," the paramedics say. To reach the helicopter landing site they'll need to hike out with me on a stretcher, but to do that they will have to gather up my leg to form some semblance of a straight line.

"Is that all right?" says the one with the mustache.

"All right, yes. Considering the other options." I say. "You look a little like Randolf Mantooth on that old show, *Emergency*. Do people tell you that?"

"This will hurt," he replies, and I tell him it can't be much worse than what had already happened.

I am wrong.

All at once it seems I am above myself, observing the way blood forms a kind of adobe as it flows into the earth, the opalescence of exposed bone, the leg slung out to the side of the woman's body, which I recognize as my own. I keep asking myself, How can this be reassembled? How can this be reassembled?

People often say things like, "I was in shock when he told me it was over" or "I was in shock over how much they wanted for that piece of crap," when what they actually mean is that they are simply surprised.

"Shock," on the other hand, is not a state of mind but a real, physical syndrome. When doctors or paramedics say "shock" they are telling you that the oxygen supply to the tissues of your body, and the flow of blood returning to your heart, has been upset, cut off, disturbed.

Blood loss over time becomes the central equation. It is good to know that many parts of your body can survive for a long time without blood. Legs, for instance. During orthopedic surgery, the blood flow is clamped off for up to three hours with a hemostat (a device which looks something like shiny, needle-nosed pliers which lock) yet the cells that make up the tissue of a leg continue living. Longer than that, however, the cells begin to die, tissue becomes "nonviable," making the leg a dead thing, a condition called ischemia, an absence of oxygen. Your heart can handle a certain number of minutes without blood, but your brain can last only five minutes without a fresh supply.

Because of this order of importance, your body compensates for blood loss by prioritizing just which part needs how much, shutting off the flow to parts that aren't vital for survival. Those nonvital parts are the hands and feet, legs and arms, which turn cold and blue while what blood remains on tap gets poured into the heart, the brain and kidneys (even though, during the course of your day, the practical function of an arm or leg appears more vital than a kidney). If you keep bleeding, eventually you will "bleed out," more specifically the word is exsanguinate, but even doctors use the lay term. However it is said, it still means there's not enough blood to support even the vital organs, and so your heart stops. But Nature is an exquisite system, measuring and balancing all factors to produce the best possible outcome. In this case that means you are spared the pain of cardiac arrest, because your brain is already comatose.

Shock is proportional to the extent of injury. The greater the injury, the greater the degree of shock. Every injury is accompanied by some degree of shock, and so should be treated promptly. This is true if it is a bee sting or a paper cut, and especially true in cases of a crushing injury and compound fracture, where there is often extensive blood loss and your body is not able to maintain circulation. Emergency workers know not to move a patient experiencing shock unnecessarily. Questions should be kept to a minimum as the risk of cardiac arrest is high, even in someone relatively young, someone with good health. A physician should be called promptly. Blood transfusion will likely be required. The *Tabers Cyclopedic Medical Dictionary* clearly states, "Constant kindly, tactful encouragement and extreme gentleness in all procedures are of importance."

I think I know why most concepts of God talk about a being from above, why angels are said to fly down to humans from the heavens. It is because when you are seriously wounded you are usually lying prone and see the world from that vantage point. Your sense of proportion has changed, so the people who come to your aide appear larger, descend toward you out of you-have-no-idea-where, and they are powerful, so powerful, so able to do for you that which you are unable to do for yourself.

Then there is the sky, which in the case of Malibu on a September late afternoon contains not one cloud. It is a blue so smooth it seems ceramic. A tint like pink or orange is quickly diluting the color. I am able to turn my head to see hands holding the stretcher and I realize this is the way pallbearers hold a coffin, and it does feel like floating, something like being in an inner tube along a glassy river.

And then there is the loud clomp-clomp-clomp-whirl of what I know is a helicopter, because it sounds just exactly like the helicopter always sounds in movies about Vietnam, soldiers trying to talk through the noise. I think I should brace for the force of air, that's what they have to do in the movies, but not that much wind hits my skin. Someone puts a hand to my forehead, holds my hair back so it doesn't fly in my face. Measures of comfort have relative value; what in other times would seem just a courtesy now becomes nothing less than evidence of humanity's central beauty.

Inside the helicopter I can't hear the paramedic, but I can see his mouth moving. His face is directly above me. His eyelashes are blond. He has on a helmet. The words he mouths are, Can you hold up this bag? And I realize it is for an IV, and I say yes because I am forgetting that my left arm is hurt. That doesn't matter because just then my body starts to shake, my teeth chattering so much I think I might break the enamel. I say, I'm sorry, but I'm just too cold.

He mouths, That's OK, here, let's get you some blankets. He pulls them up to my chin as if tucking me in. I would sleep if there were not the feeling of being gnawed upon, bitten into, through every part of me but the last eighth, a sixteenth maybe. The lack of pain there more terrible. I close my eyes but I see again the picture of Harley's stomach above me. The V shape of muscle on the underside, the never-seen side, is tattooed on my lids. The skin quivers, the hind leg cocking up, then striking down. It occurs to me that when this was happening, it already felt like a memory. I knew the blunt force that was to come, a remembered weight on me. Some primal recall from the reptilian part of my brain, from a time before the cocoon of civilization. Our species is, after all, fleshy, no exoskeleton, used to being struck underfoot.

From then on I try to keep my eyes opened to that space above me, the one through which help keeps arriving. I try not even to blink.

"I've never been in a helicopter," I say, although I might only think it.

The blond paramedic comes into view. He gives me a thumbs up, shouting, "We're over the water. Almost there." He means the helicopter is flying over Santa Monica Bay, and within minutes will reach inland to Westwood, and then to the roof of UCLA Hospital.

My jaw will not stop its rattle, my lungs won't give me enough air to shout back to him. Still, I try. "Flying sure beats the hell out of rush hour on the PCH," I say. The tradition in my family is: The more fear, the more swagger.

The paramedic nods, pats my good shoulder. He has no idea what I just said.

There doesn't seem to be any warning when we land. The helicopter is not like a plane where the sense of deceleration is obvious, or perhaps it is obvious, but my body is too busy registering other feelings and can't be bothered with one more thing. I know we are on the ground because the doors open. The paramedic says "Good luck," and then people in white coats, in blue smocks, fill the space above me, transfer me to a gurney. Talk, talk, talk. I can't get a grip on the information they're trading until one says, "Samantha? I'm Dr. Etmanon. How are you?"

"I'm fine, thanks, and you?" Always be polite, my eyes searching until they find the face the voice belongs to. He has glasses, a square jaw, chest hair peaks out of the neck on his smock.

"I bet people call you Sam."

"I bet people just call you doctor."

"Not my mother," says Dr. Etmanon. He tells me I have been seriously injured, that I will need to go to surgery as soon as they "assess the extent of my injuries."

"It's just my leg, everything else is fine," I insist, not mentioning the shoulder, it doesn't count, it's still under my skin. It's always best to split the difference in these circumstances, I have learned. Don't give anybody too much to worry about. People are easily overwhelmed.

He continues as if I never spoke, explaining that an orthopedic surgeon will take care of my bone, and then there will be a vascular surgeon to deal with the problem of the arteries and veins. There might be others; I lose track.

"All the king's horses and all the king's men," I say.

He asks me about pain, do I have any, and when I say yes he seems glad, as if I could have answered otherwise. Everyone seems to be walking very fast but he keeps asking me questions in a calm, measured voice. Do I know what day it is? Monday. Do I know what month it is? September. Year? 1997. Who's the president? Clinton, and I voted for him twice because he plays sax and likes McDonalds.

I know the reason he's quizzing me; inappropriate answers can be a sign of brain injury, trauma to the skull otherwise not seen. One of my first magazine jobs was at *Emergency Medical Services* magazine. I got fired. I was a worthless copy editor; still, you learn a few things. But who really taught me this was my mother, a nurse with a specialty in ER and operating room. I grew up with the smell of antiseptic; at home we used a surgical steel hip prosthesis as a paperweight. At dinner she once passed me the plate of boiled cauliflower and said, That's what your brains look like. When I said Yuck in my 8-year-old way, she was bewildered. She'd been on call for the past 14 hours. *What's the matter with you? It's just brains, for chrissake.*

I am telling Dr. Etmanon this story. He has gone out of my sphere of vision, but I keep talking. By now the gurney has stopped; I seem to be in a waiting room. "Plus I've had a few concussions over the years," I add.

"Horses?" he asks, popping into view.

"Horses," I say, and he shakes his head.

Above me the space is filled with white ceiling tile, the '70s kind with holes patterned through it. Some of the tiles bear amoebae-like, brown stains. Did something drip down or spray up? What would be spraying up, I wonder? Some of the tiles are torn at the corners, one is missing, there are marks on the walls, the hospital seems used, slightly bombed out, a Beirut quality. I start to panic—What are they going to do to me here? I'll ask to be taken somewhere else—and then it hits me, this isn't a menu, I don't have a choice.

"What do you do, Sam?" says Dr. Etmanon, the tone like he's making conversation at a cocktail mixer, then in the next breath he yells at someone to get such-and-such ready, Tell them I need it NOW! We're going on hour three! His head turns back to me.

"I'm a writer," I tell him, and my teeth start to chatter again. I am thinking what "hour three" could mean. What are the factors that go into telling time in a hospital?

"Great! TV? screenwriter?"

"Books and articles. The kind that doesn't make any money." I have used this line many times in Los Angeles. It comes out with no effort, even through the clacking of my teeth.

"Well maybe you can write about this and it can be your first script," he says encouragingly.

"My big break," I say.

"'Break,' very good. You're a professional, I can tell."

"Don't try this at home."

I can hear my own voice falter. Pain arrives in a series of bolts; the moment one subsides, another arrives. "I don't mean to complain, but can I get something for pain?"

I know he's going to say no, which he does, because painkillers can mask symptoms of other things that could be wrong. He says we're waiting for the X-ray department. He keeps looks at his watch. "Let me go check," he says. "I'll be back."

A parade of smocks follow; some introduce themselves, some don't, each has some medical function and each seems to need to lift up the blanket covering me and see the leg. They are not shy with their comments.

"Wow!"

"Ouch."

I joke that I'm going to start charging admission if one more person looks at the leg. I feel like a roadside attraction.

A doctor with a long ponytail the color of sand leans over my gurney. She is telling me something in a loud, slow voice, and I want to say, My horse broke my leg, not my eardrums.

She asks me if I have any questions, although I haven't any idea what she just said.

"Will I be able to walk again?" I quickly change the question when I see the look on her face. "At least ride?"

"Don't count on it." She puts away without saying anything else. She reminds me of the third grade teacher who threw erasers at me when I kept repeating the same incorrect answers to my multiplication tables. Sandy Ponytail becomes the enemy, and I feel a flush of energy. Clearly it is more pleasant to hate than to fear.

"Nice meeting you, Miss Congeni-fucking-ality," I call after her, but my voice is not loud.

No one comes for several minutes. There is no way to be comfortable, no possibility to move. I think of the ache that comes whenever I bite into anything cold; my entire body now feels like that.

Another woman who doesn't introduce herself fills the space. She has a clipboard, she wants to know if I remember my insurance number, if I could sign this release form please, and this form, too, and just this one more, right there, yes, and on the back.

I want to be helpful, but it is difficult to hold a pen. I tell her I'm left handed and that arm is numb from having the shoulder popped out and then in again, and I'm shaking because it's so cold. She seems not to mind that my signature isn't too well formed. "And we are calling this person you have listed, is he a friend or a relative?" she asks.

"Husband," I tell her, "that's my husband."

■ ■ ■

My chest tightens. There is more I want to say about him. His name is Matt. I have known him since I was eighteen, since he was sixteen. He's the younger brother of one of my best friends from college.

Now Matt will be sitting in front of the recording console at his new job, and he will answer the phone. It will be a hospital clerk telling him I have been in an accident, and he will say she's been in accidents before, I'll pick her up after work, and the clerk will say, no, she's going to need to stay in the hospital for a bit, and then—

And then I don't know what he'll do.

Will he slam the phone down, be angry that he has to leave work when he is trying to make a good impression on his new employer? Or will he feel anxious, imagine the worst possible thing that could happen, grab his keys and run out to the parking lot? What for him would be the worst possible thing? Death of a wife or paralysis, forever dependent? Maybe he will rush to the hospital and gun the accelerator through stoplights. Maybe he will need a cigarette and pull out the ashtray in the truck, and a joint from before will fall out, he'd forgotten he'd stashed it there in the back. Maybe he'll look at it and think What the hell, perfect timing, and maybe he'll light it and then decide he needs another one. Then instead of going straight to the hospital maybe he'll think he should just swing by that guy's house, the guy from before, you know the one. Maybe he'll think to himself, It won't take very long and damned if I can face this shit this straight.

I feel suddenly as if my gurney has one wheel tilting off the edge of a cliff, clumps of soil crumbling underneath the way the ground does in California. I want to tell the woman with the clipboard to make sure he understands that I'm OK, insurance will cover this, I'll come home and everything will be fine, the only thing is, for a while he'll probably need to take the dogs out in the morning. Otherwise everything will be fine. I'll just need a few days to rest.

But the woman with the clipboard has already left.

■ ■ ■

A group of people surround me, among them a doctor whose name I don't catch. I am going into surgery shortly, they say. I am so cold, but I try not to shiver. I start talking, trying to be funny, I think it's the Monty Python "Holy Grail" routine where the black knight, upon having his limbs whacked off, keeps repeating, "It's only a flesh wound! It's only a flesh wound!" I truly don't know what I am saying, but I do see the whites of their teeth, hear them surprised by their own laughter.

From among the heads peering in at the space above me there is suddenly a hairline I recognize. He arrived so quickly. His hazel eyes are clear, focused, he's wearing a shirt I bought him, green with a collar and stripes down the front, I thought it was cool. I think he hates it but wears it anyway. Tears sting behind my eyes and for the first time I think I will cry.

"Hey babe," Matt says, bending down to kiss me. There is no panic in his voice, just calm. "Are you OK?" He moves a hand to my cheek, and rubs away what must have been a streak of mud. I become aware of the sandy dirt crusting my scalp.

"I did it this time," I don't want to let go of his hand. He must be saying something but I don't know what, just conscious of the fact that he is standing next to the gurney.

I hear Dr. Etmanon's voice in the room, he's talking fast again, there are many things he needs to have other people do for him Right Now. His hands move quickly, gripping the gurney and his voice is edgy, says we are going to X-ray. Matt can't come, he has to stay in the waiting room, so just as quickly as I saw him I am without him again, traveling down a hall with greenish light.

The gurney stops at X-ray; the room is dark and colder still. Dr. Etmanon tells the lab tech he wants film on—what? My neck? I can't hear him. The break? I don't know why, you can see the cross-section of bone by just lifting the cover off the splint. "I'll be back in a couple minutes," he tells me.

These couple minutes hang like something wet. The lab tech moves slowly compared to the paramedics, the nurses and doctors. His English is thickly accented; I don't know which Asian country he is from. Maybe it's Vietnam, maybe Cambodia. He's thinking to himself, Americans complain so much because they can't believe anything bad can happen to them. Lady, you should have seen the people who had their legs blown off in my country. They didn't snivel. They didn't even have a hospital to go to. They went back to work the next day. Fed their kids.

The lab tech wants to know if I can move at all, if I can hold a plate here, over the leg. I would like to, but I am so cold, I say, And I hurt. I really, truly hurt. There is the buzz and click of the radiation burning an image on to film. Perhaps there is another one, I don't know. My brain can't handle any other message but pain, pain like I-want-to-die pain, and I recall reading about soldiers during the Civil War. When their legs were amputated all they had to comfort them was a stiff belt of rye whiskey, and now it made sense, a mangled limb for a drink of booze. A fair trade.

Dr. Etmanon comes in again. He should have wings, be named Michael, the avenger, because he always seems mad at somebody, and this time it is the lab tech. We don't have TIME. We have to get her in here. NOW. I mean it. No, that's it. Period. I don't care. We have to risk it.

The gurney is moving. A series of turns, some halls. Someone puts a cap on me. I say there's dirt in my hair. No one listens. Something must be going through my IV now because I feel a little warmer, lights appear brighter. There is a calm. I have to be moved on to a surgical table; I cannot tell how this is accomplished. A ring of faces in blue masks peer down at me. All of them are men, all of them have kind eyes.

"If I had known I'd meet so many good looking men, I would have mortally injured myself sooner," I say, probably sounding drunk. A little Mae West in the face of surgery can't hurt. There is definitely something coming though my IV.

The anesthesiologist prepares his potions. A stiff belt of rye whisky in trade. Dr. Lui introduces himself as the orthopedic surgeon. "We are going to do everything we can to save your leg." Maybe he doesn't say that, maybe I want him to say that.

■ ■ ■

I wake up in a hospital bed to find my leg swathed mummy-like in soft bandages, elevated above the level of my head, a series of tubes and needles lodged in the veins of both hands, a catheter tube taped awkwardly up my urethra. Dirt is still crusting my scalp.

I am not thinking about pain because it is just there, everywhere, the world and the filter on the world. Next to my hand is a small device like a TV remote, but with just one button. When I click it a dose of morphine is administered directly into my bloodstream through one of the tubes running into the veins of my hands. A nurse must have explained this at some point; I don't think I knew it before. I quickly figure out that after a certain number of clicks the machine won't administer any more doses, even if the pain hasn't been beaten back. Click, click, click. And still it hurts.

I close my eyes. I open my eyes. I cannot say if an hour or second is spent in between.

I become aware that Dr. Etmanon is in the blue-walled patient room. He has some information that is very important and detailed to tell me, and I believe he repeats this information many times, because I come to understand it.

"I need to explain some things to you: You have a barnyard open compound fracture of the tibia and fibula. This is a serious injury, Sam," he says. He's talking to me in a Zeus tone, as if throwing down thunder from Olympus. He doesn't look any older than I am. Younger, in fact. "Fractures are graded one through three, with three being the worst in terms of infection risk, soft tissue damage and loss of blood supply to the area. You have a Grade III."

"Top of the class," I say, although the words said out loud don't contain the confidence of the voice in my head. My lips feel numb.

Dr. Etmanon refuses my banter. "Within the class there are groupings A, B, and C. Technically a Class C, a crushed limb, is worse than what you have because the bone is pulverized and veins exploded, but the severity of this injury increases exponentially just because it was done by a hoof. That's why it's called a barnyard injury."

Barnyard, as in bucolic, as in Rebecca of Sunnybrook Farm. What am I thinking. I know better. My uncle was a rancher. My husband's grandfather, a sharecropper. I know about barnyards and all they represent, wading through the soup of mud and animal shit on rainy days, the sting of urine, the yellow bot eggs sticking to the hide on livestock, worms and other parasites. You don't even need a microscope. The barnyard has entered my body.

Dr. Etmanon is telling me the barnyard aspect is significant because it means the high risk of infection in this fracture has shot up even higher, further complicated by the fact that I lay in dirt and mud for more than an hour before the helicopter could reach me. He's telling me this injury is messy, complicated. If I had been a soldier catching shrapnel it would have been better, because the heat from a bomb would have cauterized the metal. If I had been a biker in a wreck with concrete and steel, my bones in a spiral fracture like a green twig being twisted, even that would have been better because it would be cleaner. "That's why we have you on this IV combining a very aggressive combination of antibiotics," he adds.

The needles burn and ache because they are loaded with chemicals to blast infection. Heavy artillery. "At least there's that."

"The danger," he continues, stretching the word out, day-n-ger, "is that such a high dose over a week could cause the kidneys to shut down, and permanently damage them." He keeps looking down at a clipboard, which is another weird detail that makes this seem like I am dreaming, because doctors from *Marcus Welby, MD* to *ER* have always looked down at clipboards in the exact same way. There are no emotions that haven't already been mined for thirty-minute segments on primetime. To see this familiar gesture from someone who has just said my leg could gangrene and kidneys collapse confirms

I have watched too much television.

Dr. Etmanon tells me that in the morning I will have another surgery he calls a "debridement," during which the doctors, using powerful microscopes, will attempt to completely scour the injury for all dirt and sludge and fragment of bone, any particle of which will, if left behind, cause an infection that will take my leg.

"And possibly kill me in the process?" It is easy to talk about this because I feel as if this is a story I have seen before. It's an obvious plot twist, a way of revealing character.

"We are doing everything we can to make sure that doesn't happen," he says evenly.

"I'm sorry, doctor. You missed your cue." The morphine makes me feel as if I have been encased in cotton. "You were supposed to say 'of course not" or 'that is out of the question.'"

"You lost a considerable amount of blood. The tissue damage is as serious as the bone damage in this injury," he replies. A plastic surgeon might be needed, because it could be necessary to take a graph from the latissimus dorsi, what in the gym they would call the lat muscle of my back, and use it to patch the calf. "But we will have to wait and see," he says. "I just want you to be prepared."

The good news just keeps coming.

My throat is raw from anesthesia tubes; it feels as if I have had a tonsillectomy and I start to wonder if they didn't make a mistake and take those out. But those are already out. Age ten. I had surgery in the morning and Mom brought me home at night when she got off her shift. She brought pistachio ice cream because it was her favorite and I liked it, too.

"I know this is difficult Sam, but you have to know what's going on," he says. "The injury hit below the knee at about mid-shin, which means that circulation to the area is not ideal, it's a long way from the heart," he says, still looking down. "Because an artery was severed and so many veins cut, more than half of the blood supply to the area has been permanently destroyed."

"Irreparably."

"Sorry?" He pushes his glasses up higher on his nose.

"Irreparable. That sounds better than permanent. It's a question of word choice." I just want to sleep. "I worked at *Emergency Medical Services Magazine*. My mom was an operating room nurse for half my life. I know the drill."

I hit the button for morphine. The truth about a narcotic is that it doesn't take away pain or make anything easier, but it does extract from one the ability to care, to be concerned, to give a good goddamn.

The doctor is still talking. Because Harley's hoof was a dull, imprecise tool, the largest artery in the leg, which runs in the rear of the tibia, was damaged but not severed. The vascular surgeon was able to save it.

"If not…" Dr. Etmanon says, his voice trailing off into a kind of verbal shrug.

"If not, what?" I ask, wanting him to say the words, perversely wanting everything as explicit as possible.

"If not, there would be no chance to save your leg. We would definitely have to amputate."

To amputate.

Click, click.

Samantha Dunn, 32, health and fitness editor, journalist, wife, book reader, equestrian, dog owner, recreational hiker, boxing lesson-taker, rock'n'roll aficionado, blue-jean wearer, amputee.

"As it is," he says, "there is some chance you may keep the leg."

I look at him. He says this as if it were a known fact, but this information changes the entire underpinning of the situation. I thought we were taking about the chance of losing the leg, not a chance of keeping the leg. "The leg," already not my leg. Something *other than*, *in addition to*. Now is the part where I would normally just turn and walk away from whomever or whatever presents anxiety, but I am weighed down by this *other than*. I have been hurt before but never like this. I realize I am hobbled.

And when I am formulated, sprawling on a pin
When I am pinned and wriggling on the wall.

I was seventeen when I memorized that, an exchange student to Sydney, Australia. I thought I had discovered T.S. Eliot. *Have you read him? He's really good!* What did I know. In the tiny New Mexico towns where I grew up we had no bookstores, only a ragged library and racks of paperbacks at the supermarket.

Click, click, click. I close my eyes.

■ ■ ■

There appears to be a priest at my bedside, and this frightens me. Priests mean there is a death, or exorcism, imminent. My mother called the priest, like she called the priest the morning my stepfather died in the hospital. Frank got converted and had last rites in a sort of one-stop shop. No, the emergency room called the priest. The woman in the emergency room who wanted to know about insurance also had asked me at some point, "Religion?" "Catholic," I told her, but that was purely rhetorical. If one were to have a religion, one would base it upon the mother and father's religious affiliation, and the socio-political context in which one was reared, factoring in, of course, the genetic predisposition toward papistry inherent in the Celts and the Italians, which largely constitute both sides of one's genetic history. It does not mean that since I had my leg ripped off I was expecting to see a priest. I don't even know how to say the rosary.

"Good afternoon, Samantha," he says. "God has given us a beautiful day."

Everyone in the hospital immediately calls me Samantha for some reason. Samantha is whom the phone solicitors and bill collectors ask for when they call, affording me the opportunity to reply *no habla ingles*. If people know me they call me Sam, or in the case of some very close friends and extended family—an interesting paradox there, why the most intimate friends yet the most distant blood relation choose the same appellation—it is Sammy.

His name is Father something-something Irish. I don't catch it because immediately I am seeing the picture: Butter on boiled potatoes. *A cigar, Father? Don't mind if I do, my child. God is great, let us thank him for the bounty he has given us.*

The priest presses a blue and white plastic rosary into my grasp, and I am put strangely at ease by this act. The beads are round, smooth. The priest is also round, smooth. He is so very fat. Unbelievably so. His fingers cannot bend inward to touch his own palm. There would be no way he could move such girth without thoughtful consideration about where it will land. He has literally become the church, the embodiment of it, mammoth, with many folds.

"How are you doing, my dear?" he says.

I must not be doing that well if they sent you, I say, but then again I probably don't say that. My pillows keep sliding off the bed. Maybe I ask him for assistance with them. Assistance. Roadside. Things found along the way. Hitchhiking once and a Napa Auto Parts guy picked me up. Actually, my car had run out of gas on a strip of highway outside of Carlsbad that no one ever traveled. Snakeweed literally grew out of cracks in the asphalt. The fuel gage on my Datsun never worked. The wipers didn't work on that car either, unless you pushed in the cigarette lighter. The heater made the headlights come on. The lesson is never buy a car from a man who wanted to take a crack at rewiring.

"I learned some serious voodoo driving that car."

"Excuse me, dear?" says the priest.

The Napa Auto Parts guy was quite a stand-up man. Couldn't believe there was a nineteen-year-old girl by herself on that highway on the way to nowhere. Pentecostal, I recall. Part-time preacher. I love to hear those Pentecostals talk. Sexier by leagues than the boring born-again Baptists. Pentecostals are scary, because they see everything in life containing an element of danger. The subtext is always annihilation. Everything is forever about to end. There are signs everywhere. I always thought it made sense on an emotional level, but, practically, in terms of everyday life, they are all just nuttier than fruitcakes. *Nutty as a fruitcake*. Gram always said that too.

"Samantha?" The priest pulls the curtain that is supposed to act like a wall in this hospital room. He wants to offer me a blessing and this time I really do say, "Just give me the works, Father."

He puts his hand lightly on my arm. The feather weight of his touch doesn't seem possible. Like something in a tutu. *Fantasia*. Elephants pirouette and poor little Mickey, how's he going to mop up all that water? I saw that movie with friends from elementary school in a matinee at an old theater on the Santa Fe Plaza. We went to Swenson's for ice cream after that. Mom gave me money from her purse, which was a big tooled leather extravaganza containing lipsticks and used Kleenex and change, so much change it sounded like she was wearing sleigh bells when she walked.

"Our Father," the priest begins, and I don't know the words so I just keep silent, like I did at the funeral Mass for my stepfather. I sat next to Mom, on her knees on that wooden bench in front of the pew, her hands clasped together, her head bowed, her tears falling on the wood and I thought they would probably leave stains. They had only been married for four years. Tears: the steam that rises as the happily-ever-after evaporates.

The priest at the funeral gave the call and the rest of us the response. I read mine out of the paper pamphlet provided, but my mother kept her eyes shut and answered in a strange language. I tilted my head closer to her, watching her mouth form the words. She was answering in Latin. Holy shit, I thought. My mother hasn't prayed in church since Vatican II changed the Mass to English. The act of her praying felt so private I turned my head away. How much is not known about her. I cannot even guess.

"…in your mercy, dear Lord," the priest is saying now, and it all seems so very beautiful that I start to cry. When I was a teenager I would ride my horse Gabe up to the top of Porkchop Hill, it was a mesa, really, steep sides and a level plateau, and once I was up there I would just sit and let him graze. The tiny tufts of buffalo grass, when you look close enough, are perfectly formed arrangements. A Japanese design, the way the green and bluish tone and pale yellow weave into each other. That made me cry too. And the delicate bones of my horse's leg, the slender cannon bone, the ball of the joint. All the strength and muscle come down to such fine sculpture. That also made me cry. I rode Gabe so much I came to believe my heartbeat was the sound of his hooves. I rode him until he was so tired his head hug like a dog's, and then I would get off and walk beside him. I swam with him in lakes. I would put my nose to his muzzle to breathe in the narcotic scent of alfalfa.

The priest is done with his official duty. That was fast. Nothing like Mass. "Well Samantha, you're in God's hands now. I'll be praying for you."

I move to touch his chubby hand and he lets me, his skin smooth and rubbery as a boiled egg. "Thank you, Father," I tell him.

After he leaves I finger the plastic rosary, and then I sleep, and while I sleep I know the words.

■ ■ ■

"Sammy? Sammy?" Matt's voice soft but insistent. Immediately I think there is something wrong. Something more wrong. He's sitting right near my bed and reaches to touch my fingers with his large, square hands. How is it possible that these large hands can weave sound out of six thin metal guitar strings? He would have been a natural blacksmith.

"Sammy?" He says again. Why does everyone keep saying my name? "I saw Harley. I went to the barn because I was so mad at him. I was going to kill him, but I couldn't."

I open my eyes. "What?"

He pets me in a calming motion, as if I might bolt. "I wanted to do something about you being hurt. I guess I wanted to take something out on him." His voice is reedy, as if it might crack. "But when I went there he was just standing in his pen with his head down. He looks so sad. It really seems like he knows he hurt you."

"I should never have gotten off," I say, wanting to clarify just who did what and why I am hurt. "I know better than that." This feeling is so awful. I can do nothing about anything. My world constricted to the size of a twin mattress. I start to cry again. More than I have cried in my life. I cannot wipe the tears away because the IV needles poke my hands when I try to move.

People who don't ride always blame the horse, as if the horse is the one with the kind of brain that can build pyramids in the desert and create rockets that land on the moon. Matt used to ride with me when we were first dating. He hasn't done that now in almost a decade. I haven't invited him, either. Did he not feel welcomed at the stable, is that where it started to go wrong? Now he'll be the one to have to feed the horse, and he'll figure out how much money I spend on Harley and he won't believe it and he'll blame me for being a saboteur, say, "We could buy a house on what you waste on this animal!" "We could afford a kid with what you spend here!" Or, "I could buy five new guitars for what you waste on this animal, this murderous animal that could very well make you a peg leg, and who wants a wife like that?"

I wonder if I have been talking out loud because Matt says, "Shh. Everything will be OK. Harley's fine. Drew and Janice are going to take good care of him."

I nod my head and turn the corners of my mouth up encouragingly but I am not convinced of anything. Maybe the stable owners, Drew and Janice, will not want to take care of Harley. Maybe they too will blame him. Maybe everyone will decide that I shouldn't have a horse and will take him away from me, and I will be able to do exactly nothing about it. In the span of 48 hours I have become a child once more.

We sit with silence between us, focus our attention on the television perched above the bed.

■ ■ ■

"Your mom's on the phone. She's wigged out." Matt holds the phone up near the summit of pillows where I lay my head.

"Please, can I talk to her in a little while? I just have to rest," I tell him. "Just let me close my eyes for a little bit."

Click.

It's likely Mom will call me a klutz, say, "Jesus H. Christ, Sam, what were you thinking?" or she'll laugh in that throaty, cigarette way of hers, and begin a story about one of my other accidents using the line, "That reminds me of the time you…" She has many amusing tales in her repertoire. I am making a list of all possible ones she could come up with, starting chronologically and limiting the list just to those that resulted in real physical injury requiring some level of medical attention, not just the bruises, or the scrapes and stumbles, or the near-misses. So far:

1. A split lip from falling on a wooden toy that had something to do with rabbits who ate carrots if you pulled them by a string.

2. A finger squashed by a car door when I was four and her friend Natalie felt so bad about not checking to see that my fingers were out of the way.

3. An open wound on my thigh, I think it was my thigh or was it my back, from a bite when Smoky, a neighbor's guard dog, chased me down the street.

4. A broken wrist from riding a bike with a Barbie case attached to the handle bars, which Mom insisted was a sprain until it turned purple and my grandmother said, Oh Good God, take her to the hospital, will you? So we

went in the back way and mom's doctor friend wrapped a fiberglass cast around it, which was great because I could go swimming with it.

5. A cracked rib and sternum separated from my rib cage when a player butted his head to my chest during a playground soccer game, in which the player in question turned out to be the son of a neurosurgeon my mother worked with and I think she could have had a thing going with him.

6. A concussion, my first, caused when my saddle slipped underneath my galloping horse during a gymkhana for the Santa Fe Junior Horsemen's Association where we had been in the lead until the cinch, that I hurriedly had neglected to tie the knot on, came loose.

That's the list up to age eleven, I think.

"What, honey?" says a voice that sounds very much like my mother's, and I think, how can this be? Then I realize it indeed is my mother's. Evidently at some point Matt wedged the phone's receiver between my shoulder and ear.

"My accidents," I croak into the receiver. "I was trying to remember the ones from when was a kid."

"Uh hum. My poor baby. You better get some rest," which is what I say to her when she calls at two o'clock in the afternoon and has been drinking Scorsby Scotch out of ice tea tumblers.

"Do you know what a grade three, class B tib/fib fracture is? Is barnyard a medical term?"

"Shit," she replies. She is quiet for a long time, or it could be that I fall sleep again.

"The doctor made it sound bad." I say.

"Shit." She makes that puffing sound which means she is lighting a cigarette. "You know the first thing I thought of when Matt called, don't you?" she says. She always asks questions as if she's setting up a punch line.

"Christopher Reeve?"

"Yep."

"I'm tired, Mom." My mouth is dry, and it feels like ants are marching all over my skin. The ants came all the way from that canyon in Malibu. How did the ants survive the helicopter ride? How did the ants survive the surgery? "There are ants, Mom."

"It just feels like that from the morphine. It's the way the drug plays on the nerves. There are no ants. Honey, listen to me, there are no ants."

■ ■ ■

I hear a sharp cry of pain that is not unlike the sound a dog makes if you should tromp on his paw. The room is now dark. The curtains, pulled. No one perches in the chair by my bedside and the phone is back in the cradle. To the left of me another patient is in the bed by the door. We do not know each other's names but we do know we other's ailments: She is a hip replacement and a cancer of some sort; the cancer drugs made a honeycomb of her bones and her joint cracked from the pressure of her own weight as she lay in bed. She has three young children who cry when they come to see her, no husband, they will be orphaned on her death, but she tells them, Shh, babies, everything will be fine. She is experienced in real suffering, she bears it with a strength that seems to radiate across our shared room. What she tells me, I take as irrefutable.

"Pain pretty bad?" she asks.

The yelp was mine? "Sorry, I didn't mean to wake you."

"Couldn't sleep anyway. I need more drugs." She jams the call button for the nurse. "Morphine doesn't do anything after a while, for me at least. Ask them for Dilaudid. That'll fix you right up."

I would go to meetings with Matt while he was in drug rehab, and I recall the junkies pining longingly for Dilaudid. "Opiates," they would say with all the authority of a pharmacist, "are the fucking kings of all drugs," and they would return to sucking deeply on their cigarettes, nicotine the only drug allowed them in that expensive, Ambassador-Suites-looking hospital. Experimental lab rats will happily hit the lever that feeds them the opiates until their lungs are paralyzed and they stop breathing. A rehab doctor said that during a lecture.

Click, click.

A wave of nausea. A side effect of opiates. The doctor had said that, too.

■ ■ ■

People are talking all around me but with my eyes shut I feel above them, separate from their concerns. "She's on an HMO. Which one? Kaiser?" "Did we get that transfer order from Kaiser?" "Ms. Dunn, we are just going to move you a little to your side." "We're just going to proceed with the schedule until Kaiser takes her." The last voice is Dr. Etmanon's. I open my eyes, which feels like exercise, a strenuous activity. "Sam," he says, slowly, "you're going into surgery."

He is bending over me. Black chest hair shows from out of his hospital scrubs. "What does your mother call you?" I ask him.

"Mohammed."

Name of the prophet. The Koran urges parents to teach children horse riding, swimming and good marksmanship. "Your family from Iran?"

"Good guess," he says.

"My mom and step dad worked in the Middle East for a long time." I spent a summer in Saudi Arabia when I was seventeen, and saw a prince's stable where horses with bodies like greyhounds stood on marble floors the color of snow.

He puts his hand briefly on my shoulder. "Mohammed?" I want to ask him if this is the surgery where they will take out my back muscle and put it on my leg, or if they could decide unilaterally just to prune, to hack, to cut off. But it takes too much effort.

Soon I am dreaming. I have the feeling of coming from

a cool, cave-like darkness into a bright, dry, California sun. I am on a trail that begins not far from my front door. I feel the impact first of one foot hitting the ground squarely, then the other. I can feel each part of my feet, the way my toes reflexively grab at the ground through the running shoes. My arms pump. My breath sounds loud to my ears. I keep running. I feel good.

■ ■ ■

A blanket covers me. "You're in the recovery room, Ms. Dunn, everything's fine." Fine, fine, a new kind of fine. I am coming out of anesthesia. I know my leg has not been amputated because the pain pulses, a pain worse still. I look up and see the ceiling tiles' holes; they grow bigger, the size of rabbit holes. And now I am Alice. And now I jump.

■ ■ ■

The great V of Harley's stomach. V an ornamental chevron. He is flying over me. He lands. I have to get that boot off. Damn. *And when I am pinned.*

■ ■ ■

A nurse stands facing a surgery scheduling board on the wall near me, the felt-tipped marker squealing across the white surface. The date written in black at the top: Thursday, 9/18/97. I went riding on Monday.

If this is Thursday, I had a lunch date with Valli O'Reilly, a makeup artist. Valli loves her dog, so mostly we talk about dogs, my pug and her Australian shepherd. Tuesday she is going to show me a new lineup of lip glosses; famous women wear a shade of red she invented. As the IV drips down the tube thousands of women are looking in mirrors and considering the shape of their lips, rubbing a color not like flesh into the skin of their mouths, and that yesterday or two days ago or—it is useless to contemplate when, but at some point I did the same considering of shape, the same rubbing of color.

So there Valli O'Reilly sits at a restaurant, alone, staring at a menu, she will be looking for the vegan option, checking messages on her cell phone, time she could be using to play with her dog, or to put this special red on beautiful stars to turn them yet more beautiful. But she is waiting for me. She wonders if I stood her up. She will consider that this is possible because I am nearly always late for everything. Lunches, bill paying, assignments, appointments, taxes—anything that occupies a pre-determined point of space and time.

I maintain this is due to the simple fact that I don't own a watch. I always either lose watches—forgetting them at the stable or the gym or in the car, or sometimes I just take them off at night and put them by the bed and they *simply disappear*— or the watches meet tragic ends, are stepped on, submerged in water, smashed against rocks, chewed by dogs. Others have suggested that it is a product of resistance imbedded somewhere in the psyche, an explanation I like because it makes me sound mysterious and tortured, which I prefer over what magazine editors, college professors and my mother called this habit: Carelessness, laziness, arrogance, sloth.

■ ■ ■

Time must exist; I accept this. But I cannot get a handle on it. Each moment is infinitely expandable, pressing backwards, then shooting outwards. The present: merely the resting point between.

■ ■ ■

Matt sits in a chair beside my bed, his head resting on the vinyl. He looks tired; dark circles have settled under the large, rounded, deep-set eyes.

When did they get there, where did they come from?

After all, he is only sixteen. He has long straight hair that he dyes blond, exactly like other guitar-playing boys from Albuquerque, New Mexico, who consider Led Zeppelin, Hendrix and Black Sabbath to be Bach, Beethoven and Brahms. He wakes up in the morning and drops acid, then falls back to sleep so he can wake up tripping. When the alarm clock buzzes he puts a cassette of Jimi Hendrix's version of *The Star Spangled Banner* in his stereo, picks out chords on a knockoff of a Fender guitar. He does this until he can play along with Jimi.

His hair is now black at the roots. He is driving a red Volkswagen van his ex-girlfriend had decorated with purple satin curtains. We are attending New Mexico State University in Las Cruces but have to go to El Paso, Texas, forty-five miles away, to drink in bars because down by the border no one checks IDs. I am the college newspaper editor. I am a "soc," he has never gone out with a soc before. Everyone thinks he's cute and shy but I stand close enough to him to know he keeps up a wicked running commentary under his breath. He makes me laugh, gasping-for-air, crying-it's-so-funny laughter.

"How come you never hear about gruntled employees?" he says. "If it's tourist season, why can't we shoot them? But what I really want to know is, Would the ocean be deeper if sponges didn't live there?"

He hates his computer science major, works in the concert hall as part of the stage crew, wants to go to a school in Florida to be a recording engineer.

He is completing the engineering school. I have returned to the country from a year overseas and he wants me to go to L.A. I have spent two weeks with my mother watching my stepfather die slowly in a hospital bed.

"It's like watching a car wreck on a tape loop, I bet." His voice on the phone.

"It's a horrible, horrible disease. Then there's Mom. I don't know what's going to happen when he dies."

"I was talking about your mom," he answers.

Matt also looks good without a shirt. "I'm thinking about getting a tattoo of you right here on my arm." He points to the rounded cap of his shoulder.

I am not sure of the appropriate response. "Matty, I am honored, but what if, you know, something happens with us—"

"Don't worry. I won't make it look too much like you."

Of course, I say yes to L.A.

■ ■ ■

I feel him brush a stray hair from my face. The tips of his fingers used to be callused by steel guitar strings. They are soft now. I don't remember when he stopped playing every day. "Think of it this way," he says, I see him looking at the IV stand. "I know smack heads who'd kill to score whatever you're on right now."

■ ■ ■

He is using one of his Emmys for television production as a doorstop to our bedroom. He walks into the bathroom where I am putting on mascara in front of the vanity mirror.

"I've been thinking," he says. "Forget this crap. Man, I hate TV. Dave and I are going to put a band together."

The band puts out a CD on a small label. It's great.

No one hears it.

The other guitar player quits and the bassist goes AWOL. Matt is dyeing his hair Manic Panic, a form of fuchsia. He washes his hair and, there's no way to get around saying it, it fades to pink. He spends the day with the band's drummer, sitting in our living room, a bong attached to his mouth as if it is a respirator. "We're working on songs," he says. I go to the barn.

It is Friday afternoon. It is no different than other days until Matt sees armies of spiders moving up and down the curtains. He tells me I am an assassin from the Colombian drug cartel. He figures out his boss is in a plot to steal all his money. Everything I say provides him further evidence.

"Everything's going to be OK," I approach him with arms outstretched, like moving toward something feral.

"Don't lie to me! *Don't... fucking... lie... to... me.*" He cries one minute, he stares blankly into space the next. Friday moves into Saturday moves into Sunday. I think he will kill me. Then I think, no, he will kill himself.

I call my friend, whisper into the receiver, crying, afraid he might hear and think I am contacting the cartel. *See, see! I said you were lying.* She says call the police. "Do you want me to call them? I'll call them—"

I say no, I say any moment he will snap out of his psychosis. But I'm more afraid drugs are stashed somewhere in the house and that he will be put in prison. The truth: That I will be guilty.

Did you know about your husband's drug use, Ma'am?

Well, yes, Officer.

Why didn't you stop him, Ma'am? It was your job to stop him. You do not have the right to remain silent.

■ ■ ■

It is the Monday I hear him rummaging through his desk. I sit in the kitchen, trying not to make any noise. He finds me, shows me a pamphlet for a drug rehab center. "Take me there," his voice is small. "Just please take me there."

It is the first week in rehab. He calls to tell me he wants a divorce.

It is the second week in rehab. He tells me he loves me.

It is the first month in rehab. I leave our rental on the fringe of Hollywood; a friend tells me about a ratty A-frame for rent in a Malibu canyon that's not far from a stable. "It's a five mile ride to the grocery store," I tell his parents. "Drug dealers can't find this place." They give me money to move. "We always hated where you lived," they say. "We want you to be safe."

■ ■ ■

Matt puts his lips to my forehead. "Sam? They're going to transfer you to Kaiser Hospital in Woodland Hills."

"I don't want to. Can't I just stay put?" Babies cry because that is their only defense against the world. "Can't things just be the way they are for a while?"

"Babe, you'll be home in a couple days. The night they told me about your accident I made a bed for you on the couch so you wouldn't have to climb the stairs to the bedroom. I thought it was just a broken leg. Sam? Sammy?"

■ ■ ■

Matt is sober. He is sitting on our couch, his shoulders rounded over a root beer, which he holds as if it here a bottle of Bud. His large hazel eyes look as if the weight of those long eyelashes are too heavy for the lids to hold up. His hair is buzzed short, a natural, walnut-shell shade of brown. I ask him, "What do you want for dinner?"

He looks across the room at me like I am someone he is meeting for the first time. "Don't ask me for anything, because I can't give it. I'm just barely hanging on."

Our house is built of eggshell and blown glass. No sudden movements. No loud noises. Pressure of any kind can be disastrous.

The formula for bone: Calcium, phosphorus, hydrogen and oxygen. It sounds like a simple assignment from tenth-grade chemistry, but it takes months and sometimes years for the body to concoct it once the integrity of a bone has been destroyed. In the case of a large bone like the tibia, part of the appendicular skeleton, as in appendage, as in arms and legs, there is a danger of "nonunion," to use the vernacular of the orthopedist, which is to say that what once was one now is in pieces, and those pieces, now separate, cannot get together again, no matter how much those pieces might want to, might know that it is better to be one than two.

For the treatment of serious fractures, it is common to use an external fixation device, what amounts to a steel cage around the broken area with spokes pointing inward that drill through the skin and hold the bone in place. But in a grade III fracture where the skin has been sliced, the muscles ripped apart and the arteries cut, the problem is how to stabilize the bone while the soft tissue heals. To do this doctors use an internal device called an intermedullary nail. This device is not a nail at all but a kind of rod, about the length of a ruler, made of titanium, the same metal used to make warheads. It's the only metal that seems able to handle the tremendous concussive pressure involved in standing, walking, jumping and running that is absorbed every day by the human skeleton. But even then, it is not impossible for the titanium to snap. By opening the knee and cutting the ligaments to move the knee cap to the side, doctors are able to shove this titanium rod through the center of the tibia. Then the kneecap is replaced and the rod is secured into place with devices that look not much different than Phillips screws, anchored below the knee and right above the ankle.

The problem with this technique is that infection rates are higher than with the external cages; amputation rates for Grade III fractures have been reported in some studies up to forty percent. Doctors are not gamblers and do not like to enter into any procedure with that potential for failure. But when there are no better bets, even doctors will play the odds.

Kaiser Hospital is new, with puce blankets and nurses' aides who wear flower-print smocks. Whenever I open my eyes someone is asking if she can get me anything. "Water?" "Bed pan?" "Jello?" The morphine drip has been removed and instead I am given Percodan, which takes longer to kick in but doesn't make my skin feel as if things with tiny legs are crawling over it.

The fluorescent night lights along the base of the room's walls glow, some alien chartreuse sunset. The window shows a view of night with no stars and one parking lot light. No one is in the visitor's chair, the bed next to me is empty. Voices in the hall break the silence, and then the door opens and a man walks in with a lab coat, which makes me think of mice, experimentation, testing on animals, *if I were a mouse I'd bite*. He has corn-color hair, freckles, eyes the blue of Frosted Flakes cereal boxes.

"I'm Dr. Mesna." He is mercifully free of a clipboard. "There are some things I need to go over with you."

Mesna. Transpose two letters and you have Mensa. Genius. I take this as a good sign.

"This is just a horrific injury," he begins, chronicling as Dr. Etmanon had the difficulties of infection, of compromises to blood circulation, of tissue damage, a list so long it begs a "… and a partridge in a pear tree." He speaks in a Midwestern pitch that sounds to my ear much like the Emergency Broadcast System's minute-long tone that breaks into radio programming. He has nothing good to say, objectively reporting on my injury as if he were talking to a colleague—Did you see the tib/fib in bed two? What a mess!—and this makes me feel nostalgic. It's like the sound of my mother's voice.

Mom, thank God. Mom, I... think I'm having a heart attack. I have chest pains and my left arm is numb.

Were you lifting weights or doing anything stupid like that?

I... (panting breath)... was... at... the... gym... today...

I'd make book it's Costochondritis. Cardiac arrhythmia would be unusual in a 25-year-old with no congenital heart irregularities.

What's coastal condri—

Costal. It means the cartilage in the chest wall is inflamed by overuse. It's a typical sports injury. You see it in football players all the time.

Mom, it... hur... it... hur—

It hurts. Sure it hurts, but it won't kill you. Go to the ER if you want. They'll give you a shot of adrenaline and an anti-inflammatory and tell you to lay off the exercise for a while.

Thanks Mom.

No problem. That will be $300, please.

Dr. Mesna says that unlike the surgical steel used in past years, the titanium nail is an inert metal, meaning bone will grow around and actually into it.

"Then how will you get it out?"

"We won't." He sighs. "I've had patients who get the idea they should remove their intermedullary nail. I strongly advise against it, because what we then have to do is go in again through the kneecap and try to remove the nail. It is possible to shatter the knee and create hairline fractures in the bone in the process, so you are potentially asking for worse problems by removing it."

All I can think is how I worried about the tiny piece of mesh surgeons used a few years ago to repair the hernia I gave myself from trying to do a hanging sit-up at the gym. At what point do I become bionic? Is there a proportion, a ratio that has to be established? Who decides that?

"But we're getting ahead of ourselves." Dr. Mesna doesn't require any help in his conversation. "It may not last long enough to fuse with bone. A lack of callous growth can be a real problem in this situation. The nonunion rates are significant. Amputation could turn out to be the best option, eventually."

"For whom?" It feels like I am sitting beside my own voice, listening to it say things. "Best option for whom?"

His brow furrows and I believe I can hear him thinking: She's getting uppity. One of those righteous, illogical types. Incapable of dispassionately evaluating the evidence. Soon she'll feel sorry for herself.

"A latent bone infection can arise even a year from now. I had a patient once who has been injured in World War II and forty years later he developed an infection," he says, moving down toward the foot of my bed. "The damage to the ligaments and the nerves and bones will likely prevent you from walking normally. Luckily your tibial nerve is intact, otherwise there would be no chance. Running will be an extremely unlikely probability. But the advances in prosthetics are astounding—with one of those you could run, and you could even ride a horse, if you want to do that again."

"And do you ride a lot of horses, Doctor?" I hear the voice I sit beside say.

"I just want to make you aware of all your options," he replies.

I am watching him move the blankets covering the leg, worried at his intention. I have developed a fear of being touched. Any movement triggers this image of the leg toppling off its mountain of pillows and shattering to the floor. *All the king's horses and all the king's men couldn't put Humpty together again.* Perhaps this fear sprouted out of the pain that results from any motion, even a deep inhale.

"Do you feel this?" he says, touching the toes.

I don't look at the leg. I don't want anyone else to look at it, either. "Kind of," I say. "I don't *not* feel anything, but it's more a sense of pressure."

"Uh-huh," he says, like the sound men make when they are watching television and you want to know if they liked the twice-baked potatoes you made with parmesan. "And can you move your toes at all?"

He asks this casually, but it is a serious query. If the toes are frozen, if there is no sensation at the bottom of the foot, the leg from the shin down is a dead thing, driftwood.

I look down at the toes, putty colored, a Play-Dough sculpture. When I was little my grandmother would tuck me in bed so tight I felt as if I were tied down, and I would start to loosen the ties by wiggling my toes, then my feet, finally kicking the covers free. I try, harder than I have tried in my adult life to do anything, to be that child again.

"Very good," Dr. Mesna says. "That's more than I would have expected."

Pain crackles up my body as if I have just grabbed an electric fence. He tells me he'll see me again in the morning, and again in the next week, and again, and again.

"Good night," he says, checking his wristwatch. "Sleep well."

■ ■ ■

Three a.m. must be the official Hour of Self Pity.

For once, it looks as bad as it is.

A horse with a broken leg is no longer really a horse. Its horseness contains four legs, a walk, a trot, a canter, a flat-out gallop. Motion is not separate from being. A horse that breathes and sees and feels but cannot move fast enough has already become food for cougars and wolves, birds of carrion, a curious or starving squirrel, for dogs and tabby cats, has become filets for the French and the Japanese. This is a constant in the natural equation. A shark that can't swim enough to move water through its gills is already a dead fish. A Grizzly with a wounded paw is a bear about to be eviscerated by other bears.

No one but me seems to be thinking about these things. I was born in the right part of the right decade in the right century to the right species that holds the top order on the food chain. In fact, as an amputee I will have no quotidian concern; so many function with wheelchairs and walkers, access to almost everything has been made equal. Look at the success stories! *People* magazine. Quadriplegics. Paraplegics. On *Oprah*, a double amputee who runs marathons (marathons, what most people with two good legs can't manage). A slight amputation from the knee down, on one leg? When you've got another leg? Who *cares*? The horse didn't step on your face, thank God. Carry a whip when you ride a horse and even the horse won't know you don't have a leg. In public wear a long skirt, always, and high boots. Pants with a wide cut can work. Avoid swimsuits, and shorts, and no one will ever be made uncomfortable by your amputation.

Men won't mind. Doesn't interfere with the ability to

have sex. Think about it: During sex, what guy has ever had occasion to look at the part of the leg that will be missing? In fact it might be good to have it out of the way. Even that is theoretical because you're married, and he's in a forever contract to you, one leg or two, no matter.

But I know my horseness.

■ ■ ■

I was not more than four years old when, one weekend, it had to be in the autumn, the leaves mustard and rust, I stepped out the back door to make my way all by myself to my cousins' house. They lived two miles away on Maple Place, which made me think of syrup and pancakes. I don't recall what prompted my expedition. Maybe there had been an argument between the adults in my house, maybe I said *No mommy, YOU shut up* and my mouth had been washed out with Safeguard soap, or maybe my mother was just exhausted from working and going to night school, my grandmother in the kitchen doing dishes or in the back yard filling the bird feeder. For whatever reason, no adult saw a child with strawberry blond pigtails and a blue sweater walking alone on the shoulder of a heavily trafficked two-lane road, or witnessed how she crossed it, or saw her travel four blocks down a sidewalk to the clapboard house where the white paint had worn to a shabby gray. All I recall is watching my own feet in tan moccasins skip over the lines in the sidewalk. Sometimes I would stop and hop over a line, pretending it was a snake that would bite me if I didn't jump high enough. I looked up through a tree, how the leaves seemed to be yellow tassels waving down at me, and how when I started up long enough it seemed as if the tree and all the leaves were moving down toward me, or that I was moving up into it, and beyond that a sky puffy with clouds.

Finally I reached my cousins' porch and knocked on their front door, thinking something about cookies. There were always cookies for me at their house. And my Uncle Mutt had a mustache. He picked me up, he had a big, pillowy stomach, and I put my cheek next to his rough lips. My Aunt Marietta dialed the phone, which was black, and simply said, "She's here." Mutt told Marietta, "Tell them to leave her a while. She must have wanted to come all this way. Tell them I'll have John drive her back."

My cousin Johnny had green eyes and a head full of dark brown hair and I loved him. He drove a blue Mustang convertible and when he sat me in the bucket seat he slide the seat belt over me and clicked it into place. He had been to Vietnam, whenever that was, and he as we drove he sang "Oh Suzy Q, oh Suzy Q, oh Suzy Q baby I love you, Suzy Q," changing the second chorus to, "Oh Sammy Q/Baby I love/ Sammy Q."

When we pulled up in the driveway my mother seemed to lunge for the car, sliding me right through the seat belt without unhooking the buckle and enfolding me in her arms so tight I struggle against her, certain I'd be smothered. Her face was wet. "Don't ever do that again, honey," she seemed mad and sad at the same time. She told Johnny she thought I was playing with my Palomino rocking horse in the dining room. But then she realized the house contained a quietness no house with children ever has.

When she called for me and there was no answer, she and my grandmother didn't even have time to yell at each other, they only began tearing apart the house. I wasn't in the yard, or the closet, or the bedroom, or the other bedroom, or the bathroom where I usually climbed up on the sink to rummage through the cabinet looking for the grown ups' makeup to play with. By the time Aunt Marietta called to say I was safely in their kitchen, Mom and the neighbors were wading in the creek in back of the house, certain I had drowned. My grandmother was in her bedroom, crying, thinking she's never get to see me become Miss America or even a Girl Scout.

Mom kept the back door locked after that. Soon I was old enough to open any door any time I felt like it, but we had moved to New Mexico by then, and there was nothing to run to except open country. There are entire years of my life I do not remember being indoors except during school. I do remember the sand of the arroyo under my feet, in winter how the red mud caked into bricks around my boots. Stag-horn cactus pierced my jeans but then there were times magenta flowers decked its crooked arms, the blossoms vivid but without scent, like paper mache piñatas. In the fall, when you shook a piñon tree, nuts fell from its cones in a brown hail. I'd bring them back to my grandmother to roast and salt in the oven. I remember the fish-scale color of early weekend mornings, getting up to ride my horse, finding an opening or making one in the fence onto the Bureau of Land Management's vast holdings. If worst came to worst and we couldn't get around a fence, Gabe would jump the cattle guard on the road, the danger of his hoof getting caught in the open metal grate always made me hold my breath. Somehow we always found a way onto the blond waves of the llano, the burnt mesas and arroyos and pine-scented hills. We would travel for hours. I'd come home more deeply freckled, lips chapped, bruises running down the inside of my legs from the seam of my jeans.

When I was thirteen we moved into a house far outside the limits of Las Vegas, New Mexico, which is nothing like Las Vegas, Nevada. It is a place of juncture, a Northern New Mexico village wedged at the point where the Rocky Mountains meet the Great Plains, a point on the Santa Fe Trail later carved up by the railroad. It is the place people conjure when they imagine the Old West. Most of the thirteen thousand residents trace their roots to the Spanish settlers who came after the conquistadors, to the mestizos who slept with Apaches and Comanches, or to the yankees who came later in the 1800s with the railroad. And then there were we, connected to nothing, three strangers hovering on the land. We were escaping Santa Fe, where we had lived in an apartment and then a beautiful adobe house where the walls turned orange with every sunset. But the rent was too high, finally impossible. Debts caught up with my mom.

The rent on the Las Vegas house was low enough for my mother to afford but the landlord left gutted Chevys, broken pickups and tires from cars long wrecked in the yard. The kitchen was painted lime green and my room had a rainbow mural covering all four walls but only one tiny window, more like a porthole. The carpet smelled of dog piss. Soon after we moved in, friends of my grandmother's from back east called to say they were passing through in their RV and wanted to come for a visit.

"Oh, that's too bad, but we're going to be away this weekend." I can still hear my grandmother's voice on the phone. Gram had been in a sorority in high school. She had worked for thirty years as a buyer for a department store. She drew exact lines between white trash and respectable people. The cars put us clearly over more than one of her lines. "No, it's impossible to change our plans. I know you don't get out this way much. It's been eleven years, that's right. Too bad, really. I feel bad about it, I do, but it can't be helped."

She cried when she got off the phone. I tried to put my arm around her. She shrugged it off. *Jesus H. Christ almighty, I would rather drop dead than have them see this.*

I volunteered to clean up, I would start with my room. But the yard, that worried me. Maybe we could rig something where we'd hitch Gabe up to one of the old cars and he's pull it out and we could roll it off the property? Or at least move it so it wasn't in the front yard. She pretended as if I hadn't said anything.

My mother refused to feel sorry for her. "If you'd get a job we could live somewhere else," she said, to which my grandmother replied, "I worked all my life and you owe me," or "Someone has to take care of Sam" or "Go to hell." It was a litany I memorized.

The only good thing about that house was the pasture on the side, a half acre of grass and alfalfa. Mom and I moved a bathtub from the yard and used it as a watering trough for Gabe. We kept sweet feed and bran in metal garbage cans on the carport, safe from the rain. In the middle of the night I would slip out and find him in the pasture, sit on the ground and watch him graze. Sometimes I would lay down near him as he stood dozing, the breath he blew on me smelled of molasses and oats and corn. Pretty soon I wasn't sleeping at all, and I would obsessively walk around the house in the middle of the night, crying for I don't know what. I thought about Santa Fe, I pretended to be in a Judith Krantz novel where the heroine goes to Paris and becomes both beautiful and so rich everyone forgets how ugly and ignored she had been before. I would pretend to speak foreign languages, spending hours inventing syntax for tongues that did not exist. I memorized the names for all manner of horse, beginning with Andalusian, Appaloosa, Ardennais, Arabian, Barb, Brabant, Cleveland Bay, Cob, Connemara, and ending with Quarter Horse, Saddlebred, Thoroughbred, Trakehner, Yakut, zebra. I would wake up the dog and brush her with my mother's hairbrush. I would take a shower, and while I was still wet I would turn the water back on and take another one. I would do sit ups until I felt a rug burn on my tailbone. I wrote really, really corny poems on blue-lined loose-leaf paper and stuck them in the spines of books. I would leave all the lights off. When not disturbed by a flashlight, the human eye can have sensitive night vision; the secret is not to look directly at any one thing but to take it all in to find your way.

"She doesn't think anybody notices her Lady MacBeth routine. I think she's cracking up," I heard my grandmother tell my mom.

"It's just puberty," my mom said.

Gram told her she was wrong. "You've got to do something, I swear to Christ."

So they put me on a Greyhound bus to Washington State to spend three weeks on my Aunt Gay and Uncle Roy's ranch. I could spend all day down at the Stillaguamish River if I wanted to, ride with my uncle in his jeep as he checked on the cattle in the evening. Aunt Gay made pancakes or French toast every morning and at night strawberry shortcake with whipped cream and Bisquick biscuits. I helped my aunt pick apples and pull weeds, sometimes we went to the grocery store in town. For my 14th birthday she bought a cake from the Blue Bird Bakery and my uncle had three pieces. Every night I fell asleep, exhausted.

■ ■ ■

What is needed in hospitals is a swivel-pedestal thing on which a phone can be located, doing away with the need to painfully reach over the banister to the bedside table, extract the phone from its cradle and bring it to the ear, a process which spans the time of ten rings.

"Hello?" I say.

"Were you sleeping?" it is a former editor and friend who is always in so much of a hurry he has edited "hello" from his vocabulary as an unnecessary lead-in.

"No. I just sound like that now."

"Listen, you need to shoot that fucking horse."

"That's a cliché."

"I'm serious. How many times are you going to get hurt? This is redundant. Enough already."

"Are you trying to tell me you love me? That you're worried about me? I am so moved."

"Whatever. Call me if you need anything. And get rid of that stupid animal. You're too old to have a pony."

When he hangs up I lay the receiver on the puce blanket. By the time the nurse comes in, a sharp series of beeps blares from the receiver. She kindly puts it back in its cradle.

■ ■ ■

When I got back from Washington, a couple of the cars had been removed from the yard and Gram had gotten the dog piss smell out of the carpet. The Encinias family, our nearest neighbors, had bought a new horse, a leggy gray mare named Linda which their eighteen-year-old son Gene came out from town to ride. He said hello to me while I was walking through the pasture with my saddle, a carrot in my pocket to bribe my horse into standing still for the cinch. I pretended I didn't hear him. He had just graduated from high school, he drove a car, he could not possibly have meant to talk to me.

A little while later as Gabe and I ambled down the dirt road toward Lake McAllister the clacking of hooves on the hard ground made us both turn. Gene rode the mare bareback, his hands loose on the reins, his back straight as if the top of his head was pulled skyward on an invisible string.

"Hey, you don't talk to your neighbors or what?" He said. His teeth were white and a down-like fuzz springing from his upper lip suggested a mustache. "Odalay, you all stuck up or something?"

"Not even," I said, in the northern New Mexico Spanish cadence I had learned to mimic. I didn't know what else to say.

"So, you know my horse's name? It's Linda," he said, pronouncing it the Spanish way, leen-da. "You know that means beautiful? Like you. Que linda."

I felt broadsided, I didn't know how to respond. "Shut up," was the only thing I could think of. "Does that nag run?" I slapped Gabe's side and the horse bolted forward. His horse shied and I thought he would fall, but he recovered and galloped that mare to catch up to us. I remember the feeling of the wind so strong it seemed to suck the air out of my lungs, the two of us laughing, crazy with speed. The horses were tired when we walked back from the lake. Gene reached over to put his hand on the cantle of my saddle.

From then on every day after I got home from school Gene happened to be at his parents' house. He rode Linda bareback over so many miles he wore a hole in his jeans and a sore on her back where no hair grew. We would sit on a picnic bench at the lake and in my head I would pretend we were pioneers with no house to go back to, just Apache land in front of us and we would ride all the way to the ocean. The first time he kissed me his hands smelled like the eucalyptus of Absorbine

Jr., the lineament he'd massaged into Linda's legs when she came up lame that day.

When the snow came and we couldn't ride, we drove in his car, a Mercury Comet with blue vinyl seats. With the thaw he taught me to drive on the dirt roads and in the Safeway parking lot. Now I was mobile. I could go all the way to Santa Fe if I needed to. I would never be stuck in that house again.

I talked Gene into joining the Army with persuasive techniques I was learning as a Model United Nations team member in high school. My argument began with a plea to fulfill his potential as a one-time honor roll designate for West Las Vegas High, followed by a reasoning that he would be entitled to a free education, which would translate into a higher standard of living. When none of this moved him I switched to scare tactics, saying he'd never be able to earn a promotion from bag boy to produce manager at Safeway unless he did something. Still, he avoided the recruitment office. At that point I sent him one of my "theme poems" explaining that I had to get out, so if he wanted to be with me he'd have to find a way to escape, too. He said the poem made him sad, but that he thought I was exaggerating.

It was time to pull out the big gun. "My mother was in the Air Force for four years," I spit out the words. "Are you telling me you're afraid to do something *a woman has already done?*"

The Army sent him to Mississippi for basic training, his first trip outside the state. He sent me letters and a wooden cross on which he carved Te Amo Sam. He told me he wanted to marry me when I got out of high school, he could wait the three years. He was sure I would change my mind about wanting to see Europe, or, he suggested, we could see it together. After that we could come back and live on some property next to his father out by the lake. He wrote that he would always be with me, and as I read I felt as if I were being pushed into a bag and watching the drawn string pulled tight.

While Gene was away we moved into a newer, nicer

house that only needed a fresh paint job and was closer into town. When he came back he knocked on the front door, and although my grandmother invited him in warmly, I walked right past him with just a hello, and I ran down the steps to the school bus. After class he waited outside in the parking lot.

"¿Qué paso?" he wanted to know, "Mira, I still love you…"

"I can't, please," I told him, not breaking my stride. He had to get up and walk to continue the conversation, but all I could tell him was sorry. I kept walking. My legs were longer than his. He stopped. I walked faster.

■ ■ ■

All I want is to be able to wash my hair. I have grown accustomed to being able only to sleep on my back, I have grown accustomed to the occupational therapists who come in twice a day and have me stand up with a walker, and the way I feel like passing out as soon as I am able to balance on my one good leg. But it has been six days since my accident and I cannot grow accustomed to the dirt from the canyon that still grates on my scalp, like the sharp dust off an emery board.

I am getting strong enough to travel the five feet from my bed to the bathroom. I am not supposed to go in there without help from an aide, because I might faint or slip on the tiles. Those dangers do scare me, I know they are real, but I make the trek by myself anyway. It's not that I am embarrassed about going to the bathroom in front of another person, although before the accident I would have been. I am not embarrassed now because they are not seeing me, they are seeing a leg, an arm, a shoulder, a haunch, parts of something totally organic and biological. I, meanwhile, reside in a small space located at my forehead that extends into my skull at an immeasurable depth. I, me, the person I am, cannot be seen, so these details concerning the body do not matter. I am bothered by the dirt in my scalp because it is closest to where I reside.

I stand in front of the bathroom sink in my walker. Several obstacles to washing my hair become immediately evident. The angle between the small bathroom sink and the faucet is too small for me to wedge my head between so that I can let the water run over my scalp. Another is the problem of balancing on one leg to do this; I have to have my arms for support. Then there is the fact that all the blood in my body feels like it's draining out of me again and I think I'm going to pass out.

How did the victim break her neck, Detective?

Well sir, it appears that the victim's head became lodged in the sink, she passed out, and when her one good foot slipped on the tiles the porcelain crushed her windpipe.

Fine work, Detective.

The skin has taken on a translucent texture. It seems thinner, like fabric, to be sewn upon. The eyes feel like glass beads, the face carved down, the shape of an overbite more pronounced. The nurse finds me in the bathroom examining the face in the mirror.

"Samantha, why didn't you call me? You should not be in here by yourself," the nurse scolds.

"I didn't want to bother you," I tell her, which is part of the truth. The whole truth is that nothing is more pathetic than asking for help. My Uncle Roy, who taught me to fish and to throw alfalfa off the back of the Jeep to the cows in winter pasture, shot himself in the head when I was fifteen because he discovered he had cancer and didn't, in the words of my Grandmother, want to die moaning like a dog. *Can you imagine being sick and burdening your family? God awful.* My great aunt told me he was actually clinically depressed and ran out of lithium. I told my mother what really happened. She didn't see there was a difference. Either way, she said, cancer or depression, either way, what kind of a life is that? Probably for the better. I raised you all by myself and never needed a handout from the government or anybody else, she said. No welfare Velveeta in this house, I agreed.

■ ■ ■

"Let's get you back to bed," the nurse says, steadying my waist with her hands.

Her long black hair looks thick, coarse as peppercorns. "Please, can I wash my hair?" I ask her.

She looks at me, then at the sink. Immediately she seems to understand. "Well, I don't know how we would—" she begins. "Besides, you can't get any water near your dressing—"

"Please," I ask once again, "I just can't take this dirt anymore." By this time I am feeling so faint I realize it's a losing proposition. She just barely reaches my shoulder even though I am hunched over a walker. She wears that bright flower print smock. I am afraid if I fall on her I will crush her like a pansy underfoot.

My IV jiggles as I get into bed. The veins burn and ache. "Can we ever, ever take this out?" I ask the nurse.

"One more day of antibiotics and the doctor says you're done," she replies. There is so much she has to do for me, prop the leg up on all these pillows, cover me with blankets, angle the bed just so. I thank her. I tell her I think she must be a good mom, and she smiles.

"It's time for your pain medication," she says.

"Super magic bus," I say. "Don't want to miss that."

She is reminding me about the medication because yesterday I tried taking one instead of two Percodans to wean myself off opiates, nip addiction before it could possibly bud. I was feeling noble. I once heard a story about a former junkie who was so committed to his sobriety that as he was dying of cancer he refused morphine and all other painkillers. About two hours after I took just one Percodan I appreciated just what that junkie had accomplished. I now ask for three instead of two as a matter of personal policy. She just gives me two.

■ ■ ■

She wakes me. "Samantha, you have a call from gentleman," she says as she wedges the receiver between my shoulder and ear.

"I thought I'd lost you. I called UCLA and they didn't

know where you'd been moved," says Edward Albert on the other end of the telephone. His voice sounds as if he is next to me leaning near, moving my hair with his hand so he can talk directly into my ear. "I'm glad you mentioned you'd be moving to Kaiser. I only had to figure out which one."

He was looking for me. Were my grandmother alive she would write in my scrapbook, *Edward Albert, star of Butterflies Are Free, wanted to talk to Sammy so he found the hospital where she was convalescing from surgery.* "Thank you for looking for me," I tell him, and I realize it is not the first time he has found me, and I want to think of clever words that will tell him how that makes me feel while appearing amusingly ironic and disengaged, but I cannot. What I can give the man who saved my life is my sincerity. I reach down for it, raw, fragile, and still a bit unformed. "I owe you everything. Thank you. I can't express that deeply enough."

"You don't need to. I was honored to be of service. It was profound." Maybe that is dialogue I heard in a movie once, or maybe this is dialogue he said in a movie once, or maybe he says it or says something else and this is what I hear. But whatever the order of the actual words, I believe he means what he says.

"You know there is a belief that when you save a person's life you are forever responsible for them," he tells me.

"You sure you want to sign up for that?" For lack of something better to add I change the subject. "How was Harley after the accident?"

"He stayed at our barn overnight and we made sure he ate well. Drew came with the trailer to pick him up in the morning," he tells me patiently. "You don't remember but we had this conversation before during the other two times I called. You were pretty far gone."

"I'm sorry," I reply, ashamed because I want to be present for the man who could have easily said, *No it's just a hawk crying in the canyon, I don't have time to look.*

"You sound better now," he says. "You'll be dancing

before you know it. Don't believe anything doctors tell you. You are in my thoughts and prayers."

■ ■ ■

The afternoon is warm; I can see the ripened September blue of the San Fernando Valley through the vertical window in my room. Friends drop in for visiting hours with the synchronicity of a parade. Mary Ellen brings six pair of Jockey underwear in every color, and a cotton nightie designed so that I can get it on over the IV. "Now this is more festive," she says cheerily, too cheerily perhaps. "I bought myself some too. Where's Matt?"

"Working," I say. "It's hard for him with the dogs, the commute. A new job."

"Still…" she lets the word trail off. Mary Ellen is tall and long-limbed, her salt and pepper hair cut in a perpetual wedge with thick bangs that fall to her eyebrows. She is the mother I would have had if I could have chosen to be born to a family of Talmudic scholars and lawyers.

"He really is at work," I insist.

"Of course," she says, brightly again. She wants to know what drugs they are giving me, what plan of action is being taken. She doesn't trust an HMO. "I'm not convinced this orthopedist knows what he's talking about," she says, referring to Dr. Mesna. Her son is getting his M.D. at Harvard. "I'm going to talk to Jared about this."

Mike, my former intern at a magazine, now turned editor, brings my best-known vice: Filet-o-Fish, a Diet Coke and fries from McDonald's. "Nothing like a nutritious meal," he says, putting the paper bag on the nightstand. I can't eat more than a few bites because the drugs and antibiotics have killed any appetite, but the act of unwrapping the blue paper makes me feel normal.

"Whoa, you're looking good," Mike says. He doesn't know if he should put his hands in his pockets or near the bed rail, so he nods at me encouragingly. "Really." Twenty pounds have seeped from me, my hair separates in wedges of grease, tubes run out of me, my wide hipbones stick out sharply like a milk cow's. I feel maggoty. I love him.

"You're the worst liar," I tell him.

His pale skin flushes to a shade of plum. He shrugs his shoulders and smiles. "Depends what I'm lying about."

Ann Marie and her daughter Kayla arrive after Mike leaves, bringing a body spray and powder that smells of lavender. Kayla stays in the chair farthest from the bed.

"What's the matter with *you*?" She says it like an accusation. She is six.

"Broke my leg pretty bad," I tell her. "Can I have a kiss?"

"Uhm, no, I don't think so," she tells me, squirming into the chair as if the vinyl upholstery will cuddle her. Her mother looks mortified.

"All this stuff's pretty scary," I agree. "It scares me too. But you can't catch it."

This must be the reassurance she's looking for. She navigates the bed rail with her mother's help, diving into the tide of pillows to kiss me. "Get well Auntie Sam. You're all bony. You look weird."

"Thanks, monkey butt," I tell her, bracing against the touch as if her small hands will push me shattering to the floor like some porcelain figurine. "You always say the nicest things."

■ ■ ■

I must have fallen asleep because suddenly I am waking. In the chair beside the bed sits my friend Renée, a light shining on her sleek brunette head as she leans toward the pages of a magazine, reading. She wears red lipstick and is dressed in black. She is always dressed in black, a dream in Donna Karan. Renée has large brown eyes and full lips, is the kind of beauty that belongs on a canvas. I call her the Angel of Darkness, a black-appareled seraphim who always appears in my worst moments. It was Renée who found the house in Malibu when Matt went to rehab, and has twice in the last year alone taken me to the local Emergency Clinic. Once for the slight concussion and broken coccyx from the fall over a jump, once for the ankle sprain when I fell down the flight of stairs at the house. There are other, numerous examples. She and I sat at the bedside of our friend Donald as he lay disfigured and delirious in the final stages of AIDS. She sat longer than I. Much longer. She is the kind of person who can hold misery.

"We have got to stop meeting like this."

She looks up from the page. "Hey girl. I was just thinking the same thing. How are you feeling?"

"Like shit. You?"

She arranges the blankets on the bed, wants to know the details of the accident, the course of treatment, the drugs prescribed. "Are you in pain? The minute you feel pain you tell them and make them give you something, right away."

I tell her about my new friends, morphine, Dilaudid, Percodan, Vicodin. "Probably serves me right, this whole thing," I tell her. "I should have just stayed on and not gotten off him to cross that water."

"What?" she looks at me, annoyed. "Don't tell me you think this was your fault. This was just an accident."

"Yeah, but there's a rule. Never get off. You're always safer on a horse than on the ground."

"That's absurd," she waves me off. "If you had stayed on maybe something worse would have happened. Face it, you're just accident-prone. Some people are. There's always one person who's going to bump their head or trip on the step."

"How attractive."

"It's part of your charm, my dear," she says, busy cleaning the bedside table of trash, arranging a bouquet she brought. "I also brought some cookies. Do you want a cookie?"

■ ■ ■

The nurse returns to my room. Her shift has just ended, she says. "I've been thinking," she begins tentatively. "Maybe if you can stand up for long enough I can wash your hair over the sink with a cup to pour water."

I feel like the people must feel when they open their

front door and the van from the Publishers' Clearinghouse Sweepstakes is parked outside—not sure whether to laugh or cry or just get busy cashing the check.

"If you will do that for me, I can stand as long as you need me to stand, I promise," I tell her, talking fast, as if my words can plug any crack where a change of heart could get in.

We make an awkward path to the bathroom, the nurse on one side of me. She sees how I manage the walker and IV stand by first moving the walker, then bracing my weight with one hand as I use the other to push the stand on its wheels a few inches ahead. "You shouldn't do this by yourself," she warns again.

"You're right, I know. I won't anymore," I tell her, because I am grateful and because I would not want her to get into trouble if I fell on her shift. Of course I will have to do this exact thing when I get home, but without the IV. I need practice.

Finally we arrive at the sink. I lean over and immediately feel weak, but I grip the walker as tightly as I am able. Sweat begins to gather on my brow but, beautifully, wonderfully, it is rinsed away by warm water as the nurse pours it over my head. She puts shampoo on and rubs it in with her small fingers. My hair is so dirty the shampoo won't lather. The sting of soap reaches my eyes but I don't tell her. It doesn't matter, and it might make her stop.

"Is the water too hot? How are you doing?" she says, reaching an arm around my waist as the other one pours water to rinse the soap from my hair.

"It's great, it's perfect," I tell her, although white spots have started flickering in front of my eyes. I reach a hand off my walker to touch her waist. "What's your name?"

"Sophia." She wrings the water from my hair and puts a towel over my head. "There, that's as good as it gets. Now you have to get back to bed and stay there."

"Sophia," I love the sound of it, the Greek word for wisdom, divinely inspired, the name of a Muse, of a goddess, of a movie star I wanted to look like once. "Sophia. Thank you."

"You're welcome."

"I really mean thank you. Thank you isn't big enough to tell you what I mean. What can I give you? I am going to name a cat after you. No, a child after you," I vow. I have no children but she makes me want to have a daughter so that I can tell the story of how she got her name, and how that name means complete kindness.

She smiles as she helps me back into bed. "I am glad you're happy. I just wanted to help." She produces a comb for my hair.

"Sophia, Sophia, Sophia," I say. "Sophia." I use it like a mantra.

II.

Accidents are like a fever—
they're a symptom of
something else.

A horse is a huge expense for any single mother but especially for my mother, who had been left bankrupt by a man she married when I was seven. She co-signed a loan he needed to start a flower shop; I still believed in Santa but even I wasn't surprised when he left with another man, taking the small amount of money she had inherited from a Pennsylvania relative with him. A daughter with a horse is like having a daughter plus the responsibility of an extra child who will never grow up and get a job. But selling the animal was not an option. That was never even discussed. It was always death-do-us-part.

As a consequence, I grew up understanding there was not a cycle of life but that there was a seesaw of life, rich and poor. When we were rich, my mom dug through the frozen food section at the grocery store to find lobster tails, shellfish like old snowballs, which my grandmother would then grill in the oven with bread crumbs and butter. When we were rich, we went shopping at the T, G & Y. Mom bought me new jeans and sweater sets. When we were rich, everything was possible. I went to horse shows at the rodeo grounds, ran for student body president and tried out for the track team. Mom bought Scotch with brand-name labels and remembered to turn up the volume on her auburn hair with a dye from Clairol called "Mediterranean Passion." Gram filed her fingernails into sharpened ovals and painted them pink.

When we were poor we ate potatoes and beans just like the neighbors. "One day away from being homeless, without any possibility of a future," my grandmother said and I believed her. I would stay home sick from school and reread Harlequin Romance novels she kept in a stack beside her Laz-E Boy. When we were poor and the propane tanks ran out of gas, sometimes Gram heated water on the electric stove and filled a bath for me before school.

When we were really poor the dogs were fed stale bread and milk, and my horse was turned out to pasture on a friend's ranch. I never prayed except, when we were really poor, that there would be enough grass to keep my horse from going hungry. Sometimes the prayers didn't work. Once Gabe lost so much weight the hollows above his eyes deepened into pits, his ribs appeared like the wooden seams of a shipwreck. My mother cried when she saw him, borrowed money from I don't know where to rent a pasture for $58 a month next to the Enchanted Hills Trailer Park, the last in our dismal series of Las Vegas homes. Our farrier felt sorry for us three gringas with no man and built a shed where we kept hay and which sheltered Gabe from Rocky Mountain sleet and those murderous July thunderstorms.

This is how I measured the commitment Mom had to the idea of me having a horse: She wore the same pair of black cowboy boots from the time I entered elementary school until I started college. She never bought herself anything on our spending sprees at the T, G & Y but instead waited until Aunt Gay cleaned out her closet and shipped the castoffs in cardboard boxes down to her and Gram. Our '67 station wagon doubled as a truck, hauling hay bales and grain sacks; she kept it running until 1982 when it literally cracked in half when she hit a pothole going twenty-five miles an hour, the frame rusted through, dissolving into flakes and red dust on impact. Still, I had riding lessons from the time I was old enough to sit on a horse, a fact she proudly held up to my grandmother.

"Your kid doesn't have a father, and what the hell kind of life is this?" Gram said. She had many variations of the same topic, but this was one of her favorite phrasings.

"'What the hell kind of life is this?' She has a purebred half-Arabian horse! How many kids can say that?" My mother's voice would tremble and she'd try to cover by over-enunciating her words. My mother stopped riding when she was twelve, scared by a nasty throw from a Tennessee Walker named Becky. But nothing was going to deter her daughter from riding, not if she had anything to do with it. "In case you are not aware, she belongs to the Junior Horsemen's Association. That is pretty god-damn-good, if you ask me. But, of course, you won't ask me."

Even Gram seemed to think the problem wasn't the horse so much as the lack of a man in our lives. She had all her life been a great horsewoman, or at least that's what she said. I never actually saw her on a horse, although I saw many pictures of her riding. She would point out her posture. *See, straight as a ramrod.* I do know she was good with horses, because she always knew exactly how to touch one. There was a gentleness in the lay of her fingers along their bony foreheads, along the half-moon crescents of their jaws. She made bran mashes in the winter for Gabe, an elaborate offering, chopping carrots and pouring molasses into it as if it were a gourmet oatmeal.

To Gram, how something looked was in fact what something was; appearances were never deceiving to her. Everything revealed its exact nature, meaning that whatever didn't look good, wasn't. She put butter on peanut butter and jelly sandwiches, she quartered the bread and always served the sandwich on a plate. Once when it was snowing my mother couldn't manage the drive home because the road was closed. There was next to nothing in the house to eat, we were poor that week, but Gram figured out a way to make a bowl of soup from an onion, some old spaghetti and a chicken leg she found in the back of the freezer. She put a lace tablecloth on the dining room table, served it in a rose-patterned Franciscan Wear bowl, and lit candles. I ate and she smoked a pack of Kools. "'Act as good as you look and you'll have no trouble,' that's what my own grandmother used to tell Gay, Mutt and me when we were kids." She told me this often.

How her law of aesthetics applied to my horse was this: Anything that touched him was decorated if even remotely possible. Even when we were rich we couldn't afford fancy halters, so Gabe's was a standard rope job. But then Gram got a hold of it and elaborately braided over it in blue yarn she bought at K-Mart for 49 cents a skein. She crocheted a forest green border on my saddle blanket, put tassels on the ends that bounced when I asked him to trot. She taught me that blue rinse would always get the yellow out of a white mane, and used her own Alberto VO-5 conditioner to smooth the tangles out of his tail. "Act as good as you look." She told this to my horse too, kissing the rubbery part of his nose between the two nostrils, staining his gray muzzle with her lipstick.

Mom was interested in what things actually did. She would sit by the rail at my horse shows, mirrored sunglasses obscuring her green eyes and most of her upturned nose. "Keep your heels down," she'd yell as I passed, in a throaty bass tone she must have believed was below the frequency judges' ears could register. "He's on the wrong lead!" The picture Mom carried of me in her wallet was of my first riding lesson on old Big Red, my short legs barely able to straddle the sorrel gelding's back, the length of my entire body exactly proportional to the size of his huge head. In the picture I'm wearing a red shirt tied at the waist, Big Red has one ear turned to the camera.

■ ■ ■

"I'm not driving you there. No way José," says my mother. She has taken two weeks off her job as a nursing director to come from New Mexico to stay with me; she says "visit" but really it's to act as my chauffeur for the twice-weekly appointments with Dr. Mesna since Matt has to be at work. We are returning to Malibu from the hospital and I have asked her to drop by the stable on the way home. I want to feel something organic in my fingers, feel wind press against my face and replace the smell of Betadine solution. Forget the orange stain of it on the skin when Dr. Mesna opened the bandage and I saw what was beneath, the bloated and purple flesh like a mammal drowned then beached, the crude cross stitch with thick black thread running the circumference of the thing.

"I just want him to see that I'm OK," I am pleading. I cannot believe she, of all people, cannot see the logic of this. "Please. It's been five weeks, I think. The last time he saw me I was bleeding."

"As if he cares. You can hardly sit up in the car. Don't be an idiot."

"Yes he cares," I say. "I can sleep when I get home." My life now: Sleeping, getting ready to sleep, and waking up so that I can go back to sleep.

"Do you hear anything Dr. Mesna keeps telling you about infection? Do you think he's making that up? That he just wants to hear himself talk? Well I've got news for you."

"I'm not going to roll around in the dirt. I'm just going to pet my horse."

"I think we should shoot the son of a bitch." Her voice is harsh.

"What is with you people!" It's as if someone I have never met is sitting next to me in the truck.

"Well I do. I never trusted him." She purses her lips into a bow, the red of her lipstick feathers into the lines around her mouth. "There's a reason he was a freebie from the slaughter yard."

"Oh, right." I want to make her take it back so I pellet her with guilt, my only defense. "Aren't you the mother who bought me a green-broke Arabian when I was eleven, the mother who put me bawling and shaking back on that other gelding when he ran away with me when I was, what, eight?"

She sucks in her breath. "I didn't want you to lose your nerve."

"I never have."

Mom puts both hands on the wheel, drives in the slow lane because even the vibrations from the road are torturous for me. We are only a mile or so from the stable now, driving up the Pacific Coast Highway, the burnt and stubby scrub oaks of the humpback canyons on the right, the ocean side rough and stone-colored, something more resembling gravel than water. A row of mailboxes appears, the familiar uphill turn.

"It's coming up."

She sighs in an exaggerated way that means shut up. "Gangrene. Air-born contagions."

"Like from this car, you mean?" We are in Matt's truck, a ten-year-old Toyota, a large dent on the driver's side, another in the flat bed, and the rear differential out of whack from the time it was struck by a passing trailer. My wheelchair props just so in the flatbed, Coke cans and empty potato chip bags littered around it. Cigarette burns pockmark the worn upholstery, cellophane wrappers and french fries from visits to a drive-thru wedge into the folds of the seat. Were a hand to lay across the dashboard it would disturb the mantle of dust that has turned the blue interior to tan. The leg nests in newspapers and other debris on the floor of the passenger's side.

"For Fuck's sake, Sam. If your leg rots off I am not... feeling... sorry... for... you!" Mom often yells in the way she is doing right now, spacing the words out so that each is stressed equally. The antidote is to reply in a deadpan tone, nothing for her words to refract against.

"I sure won't come running to you," I tell her.

She stares straight at the road.

"'Run,' get it?" I am talking at her profile. "*I* won't come *running*, ha-ha?"

I feel a deceleration, Mom turns the steering wheel into the driveway for the stable. She pulls up to the gated entrance, still not looking at me. "Fine. Be that way."

■ ■ ■

The iron gate to the stable creaks open slowly on its electric hinge. My eyes scan the grounds, there are a number of bays at the stable but I am looking for the distinct inky points of Harley's ears, unlike any other.

I love my horse. I don't mean I love my horse like I love Ben & Jerry's Chocolate Chip Cookie Dough Ice Cream. I mean that my relationship to Harley, a living, breathing, sentient being, is as important to me as any human friendship in my life. More than some.

Since the first week we arrived in Los Angeles, Matt was in the studio, or working on a show, or playing his own music. When we did see each other it was brief, intense, a perpetual romance, I would literally catch my breath when I saw him. For a couple years after we were married I still called him my boyfriend, we were not subject to the boredom, or the familiarity, that quotidian routines supply. With his erratic comings and goings, I too tried to work, to make it like breathing, doing something every minute. I took classes. White space on the calendar was my enemy.

Even so, for years I had felt adrift. Once on a lark I went with friends to a rental stable in Griffith Park so we could waste a summer afternoon. The smell of leather, the juxtaposing scents of sweet oats and acrid muck, the wet sound of a horse rolling the bit in his mouth. It was as if a switch inside me had been flipped on. Riding again was like having amnesia and finally remembering my own name. I couldn't wait to do it again; I immediately started hanging out at the stable, leasing horses, riding any four-legged excuse for an equine I could find a way onto.

Finally I had a way to engage my body and senses together, to get my hands dirty, to spend hours communicating and not saying a word. I started to become part of the physical world again; I woke up before sunrise just to squeeze in a ride before starting to work. I knew winter was coming because the horses' coat grew longer, that the Santa Anas were about to blow because they suddenly became restless and spooked at the wheelbarrow they saw everyday, as if it had suddenly grown fangs. Every horse that passed under my care I treated as if he were a Triple Crown winner, brushing every inch of coat, down to using a toothbrush to smooth the hairs around the coronet band of their hooves.

A woman I knew from the stables brought me a poorly Xeroxed flyer she found at the feed store. To a good home, it said. Just take over this gelding's care, period. "There's got to be something wrong with him," I thought as I stared at the picture, as if by closely examining the Xerox I would pick up the hidden message written in invisible ink. The evidence in black and white said plainly enough: Large head, skinny neck, one section of mane that seemed to grow from the wrong side. A broomstick pony. But I liked his name, Harley. It sounded rock'n'roll, all-American, tough but not unattractive. Sure, you might have to tinker with him all the time, but that was part of the experience.

The horse was stabled a half hour from L.A. in Sun Valley, where it's hot, land is cheap and residents achieve the dream of owning a suburban ranchette. People drive pick-ups and leave their dogs in the flat bed, put aluminum screens on their front doors, don't seem bothered by the dust off the dirt roads that filters in. I drove up to a house with pipe corrals in the back. It appeared the owner raised mules. Champion mules, the sign by the mailbox said.

The gate to the rear of the property was open. To the side of the barn there was a huge arena, where sand was flying up as if a small tornado were passing through. At the center of it was a bay horse bucking and running. He was huge, dwarfing the mules standing in their stalls, their long ears like antennae aimed at the ruckus being kicked up in the arena.

The owner of the champion mules walked up to me. "He just loves to run," she said, eyeing the horse, keeping a wide smile on her face as she said it. "Yeah, he sure loves to run."

I couldn't believe this was the broomstick pony. He looked like a "mighty steed" from one of the illustrations in the horse books I devoured as a child. The exact bittersweet chocolate shade of his coat, and the way it darkened to a crow's black on the legs. The straight profile and large eyes, as if the mount of Alexander the Great depicted in Greek statues has shaken off centuries. The round shoulders and forceful haunch, creating two explosive circles of power. I put my hand on the rail and he stopped dead, snaking that neck around to better view what dared disturb his enjoyment. He snorted at me. Shook his head, the mane flopping to the wrong side, and then he gave out a long sigh. He dropped his head and swung around, walking toward me with a loose, confident gait.

And, honestly, there was something about him that reminded me of meeting my husband. How years ago he's walking into that college party with a case of beer under his arm, his shirt half open, his hair long, biceps pumped, a more than passing resemblance to David Lee Roth of Van Halen fame. My best friend Tina noticed my head tilt with interest and grabbed my arm. "No way," she said. Steer clear of him; he was the younger brother of our friend John, the one who had "been in trouble." Rumors about drugs, a run-in with the cops, he was a guitar player, had a girlfriend who drove a Chevy Nova and carved his initials in her arm. "Plus, " she reminded me, "you already have a boyfriend." Matt was also three years younger than I. Matt was all wrong for me. Matt was irresistible.

I expected the horse to mooch the carrots but instead he slung his head over the rail. A deep scar cut across the bridge of his nose, the proud flesh where a gash had healed black and shiny. He stuck his tongue out about four inches, folding the slimy, bubble gum-colored thing in his teeth like a taco. Then he began to bob his head, tongue flapping against his nose.

Nothing I knew about equine behavior quite explained this. "What the hell is he doing?"

"Oh, he just likes you to pull on his tongue," said the mule owner, smile still fixed. "He's figured out he gets attention that way."

"Can I ride him?" The mule owner didn't care, he was not her horse, just a boarder at the ranchette. The woman who actually owned Harley showed up minutes later. She had rescued him from a slaughter yard; he had been a depressed heap of bones held together by a thin hide, just days away from being killed. From the tattoo on his upper lip, the mark of a purebred who has raced, she'd been able to trace his registry and racing record. The record said he's been on the track for two seasons, won one $100,000 purse then never saw success again. She'd fed him, groomed him, and had him vetted. She started riding when he was strong enough. "I just love him, he's a sweetie. But with kids and a husband, time only goes so far. You know how it is…"

"Yes," I agreed, although I didn't know how it was. For me marriage meant time stretched out in long, solitary periods. My life was more like a sand pit I was always trying to fill.

I mounted Harley. It was like being on top of an armored tank, something massive, unbending. His trot was a malformed shuffle, he held his head straight up in the air in true broomstick fashion. When we cantered it felt like I was playing giddyup, his gait tense and unyielding, not the rolling motion a relaxed animal naturally provides. All of this was evidence of physical pain. Here was a creature ground down by hard riding and abused by relentless demands. His owner's recent care couldn't erase it. He had the quality of something that had been removed from ashes, smoke damaged, edges singed and crumbled, but otherwise intact.

"Now, there are a lot of little things wrong with him," his owner told me when I dismounted, ticking off a list of cracked bones, bad joints, pulled tendons, scars and muscle injuries.

"Maybe I can put some time in to fixing him," I tried to say lightly, but my voice must have shook a little. I felt a sense of outrage and sadness for this animal. He who has no desire other than to avoid pain and just get along. He who is judged and condemned for what he cannot help but be. I stood close to his head and looked into the dark center of one large eye, trying to see if those feelings were expressed in it or if there was only the reflection of what I was putting there. It didn't matter either way. I blinked quickly because suddenly something burned in my eyes like ammonia.

"You can always give him back," the woman told me.

Even then I knew I had no intention of ever giving him back.

The sight of Harley pricking up his ears when he hears my car pull into the stable has marked my days for years now. When he hears the sound of my voice he screams for me as if I am another horse. As I groom and tack him up, I talk to him; he knickers back. It's a running conversation. If I stand brushing his forelock he'll lift his head and put his muzzle on me and rub his nose along my neck and into my hair, in imitation of the way horses groom each other. You'll see them standing in pastures sometimes like this, their large bodies facing each other, necks intertwined, using their horse lips and their horse teeth to gently scratch each other's back.

"It's amazing how much that horse adores you," Janice always says, who along with her husband Drew owns the stable. "Too bad he can't die and be reincarnated as a man. He'd be your true love."

Ours isn't a perfect match, however. Under saddle he is a difficult horse. He requires an extremely gentle hand; precise, consistent pressure with the leg. I am not naturally gentle, and I am inconsistent by his standards. He is prone to tantrums when things don't go his way. He is known to rear, and bolt, his whole front end tucking out from underneath me in a cat-like leap to the side. He bucks but not very high, more like a cow kick, off to one angle. I always carry sugar, which is a problem, because sometimes, without warning, he will simply slam on the brakes and crank his neck around to look imploringly up at me in the saddle. Such begging is not rewarded; still, he does it anyway.

But, sometimes, there is a moment when everything works. When I forget I have legs and arms and the motion of his back becomes not separate from my being. When it works I think something—turn, canter, change leads—and I blink, and in the space of time it takes to blink I am rewarded with a tremendous power that builds from underneath me, and we are launched forward. And then there is a space where no thinking occurs. It is just being and movement and a lightness I cannot describe. There is no word for it. The Greeks tried, I am convinced, and could not, and had to invent the image of Pegasus.

■ ■ ■

I hear the slam of a screen door. Drew and Janice come to the driveway to greet us, acting as if it is completely normal to help me into a wheelchair. The clarifying effects of time + distance ÷ loss of self propulsion: "Stable" is a romantic label for what is actually a sprawling series of prefabricated metal structures and pipe fencing struck at sharp right angles, lain across an uphill-slant of sandy soil and decomposed horseshit, becoming again the grass it once was. Hoses to watering troughs and animal piss cut rivulets in the dirt, and when baked by sun become impossible to cut as concrete. Drew breathes hard as he wheels my chair up the slope toward Harley's corral and my mother steadies the cotton blanket she has put over me. I have to suck in my lip because even after three Vicodin this motion is something to be endured.

Janet talks quickly, smiles. Her large eyes, the color of globes, dart here and there, her gaze landing anywhere but on my ridiculously oversized gray sweatsuit, the material on one leg cut to accommodate the bulky, wrapped column attached. She tells me they are so glad to see me, the weather's been nice, uh? Everyone is happy I'm feeling better, and oh look, here's Harley. He's been fine, really. He'll be happy to see me too. Harley? Come here, Harley.

Harley stands at the back of his corral, his haunch cocked towards us. He doesn't turn around.

"Harley, hey," I say encouragingly and try to whistle but my lips cannot form the shape.

Not even his ear flickers toward me.

The moment turns awkward. Drew, Janice and my mother stand around my chair, silent. Hands curl in my lap, two useless things.

Drew yells across the grounds to the stable's groom, Juan, asks him to put Harley in the small ring *por favor, la señora es muy trieste*. Janice goes to find a carrot, tells me not to worry. "It must be the chair," she says, and I agree, yes, the chair must scare him.

"Of course," she says, "he doesn't recognize you in it."

My mother remains silent as Drew wheels me to the side of the ring where Juan has released Harley. He ambles again to the far side of the area away from me, head down, nose tracking the scent of other horses who've used the ring that day. Looking at the sway of his large sides, the shake of muscle as he walks, I am all at once aware of how small I am and an image of a chipped teacup flashes over and over. The dust kicked up by his every step. Dr. Mesna's voice pours as through a megaphone in my head: Risk of infection.

Janice puts carrots in my hand and that Harley registers, turns his huge body toward me to cross the ring. I hold a carrot up and he swings his head over the fence, his eye only on the treat, grabbing at the carrot, attacking it with the intensity of a cat biting down on a mouse. As he jerks it from my weak grip I pull back, afraid, hating that I am afraid, embarrassed now, acutely aware of my sunken frame.

Harley turns away, distracted by the sound of another horse, me an alien being, and I realize something else was broken on that trail, a spell, a trust, something I can identify now only by its absence.

Mom says, "Honey, this is a lot for you today. Let's go."

Drew and Janice agree, yes, long day, go home and get rest. I nod because I don't know what else to say.

On the way back down the hill Drew says that he'll have Harley leased out to someone so I don't have to worry about the horse being ridden and exercised. "Just while you get well," he adds. "If you want." His voice is so casual it is too casual, and I know he must have been practicing how to say this to me. He helps my mother lift me into the truck, situating me among the litter.

■ ■ ■

Mom and I ride the remaining five miles from the stable to the house in silence. You know you're pathetic when even your own mother won't offer a sarcastic, I-told-you-so comment. Even when I start to cry she doesn't say anything, just reaches a hand over and rubs my arm.

Pain is not a physiological fact, in the view of medicine. A physiologic fact is, for instance, bleeding: Cut a vein, blood appears, and that blood will occupy space, it can be seen. Pain, however, is something the brain creates as a response to stimuli like a cut or a cancer, or like dreams or longings, like anger, like fear. The cut/bleed response is as sure as gravity, but the pain response changes based on the situation. The same stimulus that would make a person scream in one circumstance might go unnoticed in another. A report made during World war II observed that soldiers who were severely wounded in battle didn't need morphine, so elated were they that their injuries meant they would automatically be sent home and away from the front lines.

For pain to develop, the brain has to regulate the traffic of competing messages. There are only a limited number of "gates" open in the brain through which pain messages can enter the thalamus, the traffic cop of the brain. Pain messages travel along the nerves at around ninety miles an hour, or less. The more horrific the pain, the slower it moves on the path toward the brain. However, the nerves over which physical feelings of touch travel are like a high-speed rail, shooting messages into the brain at about two hundred miles an hour. This is why the natural impulse is to rub a toe that's stubbed— the touch signals beat the pain signals to the gates, so there is not as much room for the pain signals to squeeze through. The result is that a stubbed toe that is rubbed doesn't feel as bad as a stubbed toe that's not.

Inevitably, however, a certain number of pain messages will crash through the gates. When they reach the thalamus, the thalamus directs the messages over to the cortex, which is the reasoning part of the brain, and to the limbic system, which handles emotions. What takes place next is an evaluation of experience: If the pain signals are weak and the brain recognizes the situation—as in, Oh, we're on a bike, we've been on a bike before, and this is a bruise, we know what bruises are—the brain will then release the calming chemical serotonin, which relaxes the muscles around the injury. If, however, blood is flowing, if flesh is open and exposed to the world, if bone is at all visible, the brain responds to the attack with its heavy artillery: Norepinephrine, a form of adrenaline. Muscles tighten, blood flow constricts, the nerves become like tightly tuned strings waiting to sound the alarm if other attacks arise.

The brain begins to closely monitor the injured area. This hyper-vigilance means increased sensitivity, so that sensations as light as a caress translate as pain. Eventually, pain signals become cemented into the nervous system, becoming a physical part of it, just as ruts in a road become part of a road. Even years after a severe wound heals, pain can remain. It doesn't need the injury anymore. It has a life of its own.

Who am I? An invalid. What am I? An invalid. All previous definitions are no longer binding.

Identity is merely events in life taken in the aggregate; I never understood this before. I know I am an invalid because I lie on a couch instead of the bed where Matt sleeps. The bedroom is up a flight on a switchback staircase, and I cannot transport myself without the aide of a walker or crutches. Even then I cannot walk more than a dozen or so feet before needing to stop and catch my breath, my arms turned jelly, feeling the pounding of blood in the leg. I am in constant pain. More difficult to explain is the phenomenon of feeling that I am broken into pieces, my body a collection of odds and ends, so that it is impossible for me to have sensations travel through my body as if it were one thing.

My biggest effort to date was the day I returned from the hospital, made it into the bathroom with Matt's help, then positioned my walker over the scale. It took me several tries to balance just so and push off with the right foot, but finally I managed to arrange myself on the scale long enough to see it register. 126 pounds! A 24-pound loss in just under 10 days! At 5'8" I finally fit what the weight charts in *Glamour* say I should weigh. The one article I haven't written for a woman's magazine; "The Ultimate Near-Loss-of-Limb Diet: Do You *Really* Need That Leg?"

I know I am an invalid because Mary Ellen comes over and clears my closet of all clothing that is worn by a woman with two good legs: pants with narrow legs, riding breeches, skirts and dresses that fall anywhere above the ankle, platform heels, running shoes. If I were convalescing perhaps I would keep everything for that day when I will be well again, but being that I am an invalid, In Valid, the condition essentially permanent, all become donations to a woman's shelter. "Give them to someone who can wear them," I tell Mary Ellen.

From the back of the closet Mary Ellen pulls never-worn hunt boots my mother bought me for my birthday, just a month before the trail accident. The leather smells just-off-the-cow new, the obsidian sheen not dulled by dust.

"You'll want to keep these," she says.

"Why would I?" Can't she accept the facts? That I no longer have a leg that fits into the left boot? Even if the leg grows—I think of it now like a salamander tail, either it will regenerate or it won't—it will never be the same leg that fit into that boot. *Keep your heels down Sam.* Like I'll ever need to worry about that again.

She sighs aggressively, which is her way of not saying to me, "I think you're making a mistake." I turn my head into my pillow and tell her I'm worn out.

"I'll just put these back in the closet. Just in case," she says. "You can always give them away later."

I feel tragic, like a character in a Victorian novel.

Let us be shed of those dreadful reminders of happier times.
Yes, let us remove these Objects of Pain.

■ ■ ■

My physical reality has altered our shared physical reality. Matt finds us a one-level apartment, no stairs, the basement half of a duplex far up in the hills of West Malibu. The ceilings are low, the rent high. Both contribute to the cavernous mood. The floors are tile. We don't put down rugs. "You could slip," Matt explains. Books are left in boxes, no pictures get hung on the plaster walls.

I seem to remember that not so long ago the pattern

of my days was formed by caring for things, meals to cook, dogs to walk, horse to ride, plants to water. Now I don't even worry about taking the dogs out. This new place is an even farther commute from Matt's new job, so he is gone for at least 12 hours of every day, sometimes more. He has had to strip animal care to its skeleton, leaving the door to the house open so that the dogs come and go as they please. Turns out that when dogs are allowed to wander around in a somewhat rural area like this, they for the most part just stay at home anyway. A huge bowl of dry food and a trough of water keep them from going hungry.

I have a sense that I used to be very concerned about these matters—the appropriateness of care, the specific dietary needs of each animal. I cannot remember the details now because everything except the essential tools of existence has become superfluous. All that is really needed for living is a bed. This bed must be big enough to accommodate: pillows to elevate the leg; a small cooler containing prepackaged meals and drinks, although drinking very much at all can cause the need for the bathroom, a laborious process best accomplished once a day when someone else is in the house to hear if a fall has occurred; a phone; and two prescription bottles, one for stopping pain and one for inducing sleep when the pain prescription has done all it can. A window is also helpful to determined whether it is day or night, although that doesn't matter as much as I used to believe.

■ ■ ■

The dogs and I live the same. Mostly we sleep. Like them I lift my head when I hear the sound of a truck rattle up the driveway. They hear the sound of Matt's feet in the living room before I do, and are able to pick their bodies up to greet him. Then I hear him coming down the hall, then I see him by the bed. He kisses me, the cool scent of the world on him.

Then, one day, instead of coming from the front door directly to the hall, I hear him stop first in the kitchen. After some minutes I finally hear him in the hall, and at last beside the bed. He paints for me scenes from his day, mimicking dialogue of his coworkers, the people I don't know but who now know him well. I feel jealous. I want descriptions of what everyone looks like. "What about this Kim? Is Kim pretty?"

Another day in another week. Instead of coming from the front door directly to the kitchen to the hall to the bed, I hear him in the kitchen then in the hall, then in the extra bedroom. The house grows quiet again. "Matt?" I call, "Matt? Are you home?"

Silence. "Matt?" I sound shrill, I know I do. "Will you answer me, damn it?"

Silence again.

"Matt?"

I hear the squeak of his sneakers' rubber soles hitting the tile. He opens the door to the bedroom. "What?" Matt never raises his voice, the more angry or emotional he is, the quieter he becomes, until there is nothing left of his voice at all.

"I was afraid," I say, feeling so ashamed, knowing that this is exactly what every man hates, a wife who needs. Gram always said that. *The minute you need anything they'll be on the road with the nearest blonde they can find. Trust me.* "I thought maybe somebody else was in the house."

"I'm tired, Sam. I just need to chill a little. OK?" He keeps a hand on the doorknob, one foot in the hall.

I am the invalid wife he needs to steel himself against, I am the added pressure, the extra work, I am a challenge to his sobriety, white bottles of prescription narcotics within reach. I see him look at the bottles. "Have you counted them yet?" he asks.

"Yes. They're all here," I lie. When I came home from the hospital he asked me to count my pills, so that if any were missing I would know he took them, and he would then have to be made accountable. It was a strategy he must have learned in rehab. I didn't understand the logic; I don't have the power to stand, let alone the force to stop him from using. I have never had that kind of kryptonite. A small rebellion, lying to him about counting these little white pills, but it is my way to make him wrong every day.

"How was your day?" I extend the question like an offering.

He shrugs. "I'll be back in a little while," he says, closing the door.

There is no view from the window, pitch black, not the moon or even a star to brighten it. All that is reflected in the glass is the room's interior: a bed, a mound of white bandages propped on a stack of goosedown, a stick figure covered in a green blanket.

After the drop-in visits stop and the casseroles quit coming, after the helpful articles about people who cure themselves with Echinacea and green tea are read, only the phone remains. Yet there are only so many times friends can be called during any given day. I develop a grading system of whom to call more than once a day and who not to.

Grade 1s can be called frequently, will relive with me the all parts of the accident and want to know more, as in, What color was your blood? Is Edward Albert cute? How did they get that rod down your leg? Wait, what happened to your horse? Editors' and journalists' inherent inquisitiveness predisposes them to Grade 1.

Grade 2s can be called frequently but only want to cheer me up, will tolerate no self-absorption or graphic details of the accident. Matt and other family members are often Grade 2s, as are poets, fiction writers and equestrians, and editors and journalists who aren't Grade 1s.

Grade 3s are best left to once a week and are pretty cover all the other people I know. They become squeamish and even over the phone I can hear them wince at any description of pain, physical or otherwise. Grade 1s can quickly morph into grade 3s.

The length of time a friend can sustain a call usually works in inverse proportion to how close the friend was before the accident. The reason for this is that more distant acquaintances need to be caught up on the details of life surrounding the accident, where do you live now, are you still married, what are you writing. Then, in the spirit of reciprocity, I listen to the same from them. The whole exchange can consume an entire waking period before I can rightfully go back to sleep. Close friends don't need to be caught up on life, so the conversation goes too quickly, as in the case of Tina, my closest friend since I was 15, college roommate, professional colleague, a no-bullshit Grade 2:

"How are you?"

"Waiting for my leg to fall off."

"No, really, how are you?"

"The same."

"Any news from your doctor? Do you have any more surgeries scheduled?"

"Not yet."

"Can I do anything for you?"

"No, thanks."

"OK."

"OK."

"Well, I've got to run [or the phone is ringing, or someone is at the door]. I'll talk to you later."

But even with the grading system, as the weeks extend I increasingly find myself with waking time that cannot be filled with phone conversation, or with reading, or by talking to the dogs and inventing their replies. The distance thoughts roam when freed of attachment to the body cannot be measured. Words and phrases fade in and out. The static, endless. My mind has become a car radio on an AM/FM frequency, searching for a signal along one long yawn of highway in the desert. *I know it's only rock 'n roll* **once upon a midnight dreary 48 month financing!** `keep his head bent, shoulder in on the rail` **Manhattan straight up no bitters** *like it like yes I do* Admitted to God, to ourselves and to another human being the exact nature of our wrongs You are a fucking accident looking for place to happen missy *if you had stayed on maybe something worse would have happened* **Face it, you're just accident prone.**

■ ■ ■

Accident-prone. How often that label has been firmly attached to my back, a cosmic kick-me sign. Not Acts of God or natural disaster. My incidents are all about bad timing, miscalculation.

I call Angel of Darkness Renée, Grade 2, to ask the meaning. She says the phrase means just what it says.

"Is it a condition? Does the AMA have a position?"

"Doubtful," Renée says. "Why don't you look it up?"

"Everybody has accidents," I hear myself talking myself out of the possibility. "Everybody has broken a bone or something."

She considers this for a moment. "No," she says finally. "I never have. A bruise is about the worst."

This is inconceivable to me. "That's not normal," I tell her.

"Compared to you," she says. "It's more normal than you think."

I decide she is a statistical freak and hang up. I begin polling everyone on my phone list; I find sprains, a few minor breaks, one bout with thyroid cancer but I tell her that doesn't count because it's in the disease category. Even among my equestrian friends there aren't as many maiming encounters as I would have anticipated. No one besides me ever gave themselves an inguinal hernia from working out at the gym. Or had two toes broken and a severe foot sprain from being smashed against a fence by a thoroughbred just off the track. Or cracked a tooth and bloodied a nose from another horse who had a head-tossing habit. Or sustained a third-degree burn on a right ankle from a pant leg getting caught on the tailpipe of a boyfriend's motorcycle. Or sliced knuckles across the sharp stucco walls of a bar in Juarez, Mexico. That particular event produced gashes so deep I look at the scars as I type.

■ ■ ■

When Matt returns home I make my way to the one big room that serves as living and dining room and kitchen. I ask him to set up my laptop computer so I can use the Internet for research.

"Did you get an assignment?" The anticipation in his voice underlines the worry over money he is under as our sole supporter. The phone bill still has to be paid, the rent due, the board owed for the horse no longer ridden.

"Not yet," I say.

"Can you pay anything on the rent this time?" he asks. He's standing at the dining table, which is really the mail collection table, stacks of magazines, bills, other things unread covering its surface.

I begin to feel afraid in a way that doesn't make any sense. It's an honest question, he doesn't know what money I do or don't have. Our accounts have always been separate, he pays one bill and I another, our arrangement for years now. Yet I am struck by an image of Matt standing over me, a flat look in his eyes, unblinking. I have seen this exact stare directed at other people—band members, a producer who owed him $20,000, a man who cut him off on the freeway. It scares me. But now this stare is directed to me. His voice is a monotone. He tells me I have to leave because I can't make my half of the rent, I tell him I'm crippled, he says that's my problem. I wonder if I am going crazy, if I am the one with a psychotic break now, if this is how it felt to him during the hallucinations when suddenly I had been transformed into a Colombian cartel leader.

I do not have any money to offer, I haven't been able to work, I tell him. "But I will," I say. "I will soon."

"That's cool," he replies. Has he always talked to me like one of his band members, like a friend and not a wife? I can't remember now really, but in the back of my head there is a sense of a time before drug rehab and everything that led to it, when we looked at each other when we spoke.

I turn to make my way back to the bedroom, feeling weepy, feeling angry, feeling I don't know what, emotions like sludge drudged up from the bottom of a pond, decompositions of other things, now unnamable.

In bed I cover my eyes with my hands and think about two young college kids who slept in a cold bedroom one December, it must be seven years ago now. The cinderblock walls of the cheap rental like bricks of an igloo, she holding him tight, wanting that she could just crawl into his skin as they lay on the twin mattress on the linoleum floor, coats and clothes lain over the too-thin blankets. His breath like apple cider, the touch of his lips over her neck, he let her wear his sweatshirt because she was catching a cold. David Bowie's song "Heroes" played on the cheap cassette player, it was the German version, the title was the only word they understood, he hummed along. She considered them high wire acrobats, turning summersaults mid-air. They could even miss and fall, it would be all right, his net extended end to end. His father drove a Mercedes, his mother was a stockbroker. Church-going folk, roots that burrowed deep, branched out wide. She grew up in a world were people seemed always to be rappelling down the face of Everest without a safety. She clutched him more tightly and eventually fell asleep with the music on.

There comes a time when that which excited now irritates. Like one too many rides on a roller coaster, the dip and heights no longer thrill. You just wait for the slowing, finally the chance to get off.

I feel myself becoming that to him. I feel him becoming that to me.

But I don't say this out loud. Our covenant is not to speak of difficult things.

Gram always said, Start with the dictionary. For her, a concept or thing did not really exist if it didn't have a word to freeze its meaning.

I've made a makeshift table on my lap for the computer out of books and women's magazines, angled to avoid any pressure near my left side. The phone line and power cord Matt hooked up for me trail over the green bedspread. My new IV. I check the online Websters:

> ac•ci•dent-prone *adj* 1 : having a greater
> than average number of accidents 2 : having
> personality traits that predispose to accidents
> <importance of identifying *accident-prone* persons
> –*Jour. Amer. Med. Assoc.* >.

I am blue-eyed because of genetics, I am math-phobic because of bad teaching, I am red-headed because my hairdresser stands behind my refusal to accept brown hair. But I cannot pinpoint the reason this other is so.

■ ■ ■

I call my mother. "You were just born that way," she says. She is exhaling blue smoke from her menthol cigarette into the receiver, I know it by the hiss of air on the line. "What can I say. Some people are born rich. You were born a klutz."

"Is that your educated medical opinion?"

"I think it's because you're left handed," she says on an inhale. "You look at the world cock-eyed."

I consider evidence: My attempt in seventh grade to have a basketball career lasted approximately two days, when, during practice, I actually made a basket against my own team. I was turned around, I couldn't remember which side was which. The side everyone was yelling at me to run to just didn't seem like the correct direction. The world is just not ordered the way it should be. Voilà, the reason: I am left-handed.

Here I was, convinced all this time it had to do with my mother drinking gin and tonics during the hot summer months of her pregnancy, to the point she was convinced I would be immune to malaria, such were the levels of quinine water in my bloodstream. But she was right. I have never suffered from malaria.

■ ■ ■

My propensity for using the left hand over the right might explain something, although just what is hard to tell. Only 13 percent of the general population uses their left hand to write or to throw a ball or flip a light switch, and of that group, more than 50 percent of lefties are men. So to be a left-handed woman is to be a statistical oddity, the joker in the deck. The Japanese once considered left handedness in a wife sufficient grounds for divorce.

Not one researcher can definitively conclude what abnormality subtly alters the right hemisphere of the brain to create left handedness; it could be a recessive gene, birth stress, trauma *in utero*; some research points to higher testosterone levels. Groups with an elevated prevalence of sinistrality include alcoholics, architects and autistics, baseball players, criminals, Down's Syndrome children and dyslexics, lawyers, mathematicians, migraine suffers and musicians, psychotics, smokers and vegetarians. If we were dogs we would be among the lupine types, Huskys and Malamutes—prone to stray, dig holes under the fence, not good at obedience.

Wired to be difficult: is this the reason nearly every culture has taboos or prejudice against lefties? Several centuries ago the Catholic Church decreed the left-handed to be servants of Satan. The Church has since eased off that one, but the sentiment will never be uprooted because it is coded in language. In English the very word left is derived from the Old English word meaning weak or worthless. The Latin word for left is "sinister," and the Roman phrase meaning masturbation translates as "left-handed whore." In Spanish, to describe someone as clever you say *no ser zurdo*, which literally means "not left-handed."

Maybe there is a reason for negative associations; some research indicates that bad things do happen around us. One study theorized we die an average of 9 years earlier than right-handed people. Another, that we are twice as likely to have car crashes. Other morbid findings: nearly four times more likely to die of crash-related injuries, more likely to have arthritis and swollen joints, more likely to have limbs severed in mechanical accidents.

On the other hand, as it were, there are just as many studies refuting these results—findings can't be replicated, methodologies are revealed to be shoddy, premises are flimsy. Reading all these studies feels like having my palm read: The secret to my life is in my hand, but I can't decipher it myself, and help is unreliable and inconclusive.

But there could indeed be a very good physical explanation for accidents, especially if they begin occurring suddenly: It could be a brain tumor. "There could be changes in vision, hearing problems, a possible tumor in the cerebellum, the part of the brain that controls coordination," Clyde Flanagan, M.D., Ph.D., explains to me over the phone. He's a psychiatrist and director of psychoanalysis at the University of South Carolina School of Medicine who in the past I've called for articles. He's sorry to hear about my leg; for a doctor he makes a surprisingly good Grade 1.

Instantly I feel a little weaker, I sink deeper into the bed's pillows, mentally ticking off a list of symptoms. I imagine tests, the white of hospital sheets, the stream of friends who cluck in disbelief, *To think she survived the canyon only to find she has a brain tumor.* Dr. Flanagan tells me not to worry, it's unlikely I have a brain tumor. However, I might want to look into the research around attention deficit and hyperactivity disorder (ADHD). It's known as a cause of accident proneness in children because it creates impulsiveness, but it might also factor into adult problems. "Generally, accident proneness is like a fever—it's a symptom of something else," Flanagan says. "It used to be thought that you outgrew ADHD, but now the research shows a lot of adults still have it, just manifest in different ways." In some cases, he explains patiently, Ritalin, usually prescribed to help ADHD kids focus their attention, can also help adults.

When I think of ADHD all I can picture is a 12-year-old boy who can't sit still and is really good at video games. I do a self diagnostic: One thing I have always been able to do is sit still. I could never even get the hang of Pac Man, let alone Tomb Raider. I decide I don't have enough energy to be an ADHD candidate.

■ ■ ■

So what about dictionary definition number two? What kind of people are prone to accidents, and do I fit those characteristics?

■ ■ ■

"Temperament seems to be a big factor," David Schwebel, a researcher in the University of Iowa's Department of Psychology, tells me in reply to an email I send him. He assists Jodie Plumert, Ph.D., in her work on children, published in *The Journal of Experimental Child Psychology,* which tries to uncover why some continually overestimate their physical abilities and end up having accidents. They are not the kids who see the cereal box on the shelf and ask Mommy to get it down for them. They are the kids who say, if I climb on the counter I'll get it for sure. "Children who are active and think quickly, the ones that seek out new sensations, seem to have more accidents in their history. Extroversion goes along with that trait," he explains. Schwebel and Plumert see the question as one of "low inhibitory control"—the ones who get hurt don't pause to consider possible dangers associated with their actions. "It seems to be something that is fairly consistent throughout childhood and into adulthood," Schwebel tells me. Although he does add that accidents tend to decrease as a child ages.

I call a sports psychologist friend in Texas I often interview, Edd Wilbanks, to get his two cents. He says that while it is true that the older you get the fewer accidents you have, it's not always so. Edd says the "go-getter" types have very high levels of self-esteem and may think no accomplishment is too great. "They may tend to put themselves in high-risk situations just because they think they can handle it," he explains. "Nine times out of ten, the 'accidents' we see in sports are somehow behaviorally induced. Now, that doesn't mean you're crazy. It just means the choices you've made have put you in a position where you can be injured."

I like temperament as an explanation. It makes me feel rakish and cool, kind of sexy and a little dangerous, like Errol Flynn, like Mick Jagger. Better to burn out than fade away, the song goes. I tilt my head a little, turn the corners of my mouth up in a knowing smirk. *Hemingway? What a wuss.*

"As they get older," Edd continues, "these personality types will probably be successful in whatever they do, which then makes them even more sure they can push the limits. But physiologically, they eventually run up against a wall."

Then I realize there's a problem with what he's telling me: I have been running up against walls all my life.

The circumstantial evidence might suggest that I am athletic: When I was five, Uncle Roy bought me my first pony, Mickey Merry Legs. I spent a good part of my childhood hiking and fishing with my uncle. As a junior high school student, I competed with Gabe in barrel racing. In high school, I ran the 8:80 and threw discus, joined the ski club. At age sixteen

I succeeded in escaping Las Vegas as an exchange student to Australia, where I learned to scuba dive, rappel and rock climb. In college I started competing in endurance riding, regularly covering twenty-five miles in a single morning.

My pretensions to athleticism intensified when I found work as a special issues editor at *Shape* magazine. I started weight training, took boxing lessons, volunteered for assignments requiring whitewater kayaking and skeet shooting. And then there are the thousands of dollars on riding lessons.

These details do not reflect the fact that I have absolutely no athletic talent or ability. None. Zip.

I am not being modest. Even as an equestrian I am adequate, at best, even though the amount of time and money devoted to this pursuit over the course of my life should be enough to make me an Olympic hopeful for the U.S. Equestrian Team.

I tell Edd all this, expecting his usual deep insights into the manifestations of psychological disorders, symptoms, cures.

"Well Sam"—Edd only says "Well Sam" in his thick East Texas drawl when he is preparing to rib me about something— "maybe you're just not built to be an athlete."

OK, this much is true. It has something to do with my basic anatomy. I have large breasts, not the gorgeous helium-filled Amazon goddess breasts on *Baywatch* or anywhere on the west side of Los Angeles, but the real, fleshy, udder-like kind that swing when I move. I am convinced this disturbs my center of gravity, dragging me toward the ground, as if I have two magnets attached to my chest. I also have large hips and thighs that have never won a race, a little pot belly and long arms, neither of which seem capable of developing muscle, no matter how much pumping iron I do.

I have sworn off any number of activities only to wake up and do it again the next morning. I always thought that some day I would succeed at something, but, really, that is not what has always put me back in the saddle or in my running shoes. I crave the feel of wood, of iron, of the oil on horsehair, the intake of air through my nose, the sting of sweat in my eyes. I am the person who grabs the hot coal in order to know the nature of a burn. Stephen W. Hawking can divine the order of the cosmos while unable to do much more than move an eyelid, but without the kinesthetic registration of sensation, can I even think? My ideas are the result of accumulated experience. I struggle forward by feeling things first, then unraveling what they mean.

I thank Edd for his time and say goodbye. All this talk about activity has made me exhausted.

■ ■ ■

In the room the dogs Nika and Ming snore gently, the funk off their bodies filling the air. I can hear the metal sound of the hands on the clock as they move. I am hungry. I need to go to the bathroom, but I am afraid of the pain leaving the bed brings, of the possibility Nika and Ming will bump against me, that the tiles will be slick and the crutches will slide out from under me. It has happened before, all of it. Underneath the green bedspread I move hands over the body there, the sharp new angles, flesh loose and hanging, imagining the microbes growing like mold in my blood, in my bones, until the parts of me disintegrate on their own. I feel a shrinking, a moving inward, not like Errol Flynn, nothing like Mick Jagger.

Outside the window wind bends the eucalyptus, its gray-backed dagger leaves shimmering. Beyond the tree more trees, then the great blue of the Pacific meeting the sky at the horizon line.

Appointments with Dr. Mesna are down to once a week; I get ready for my first weekly trip to the medical center as if I'm preparing for an opening night appearance. The ritual takes hours. I wash my hair, now cut short to the nape, easier to wash in the bathroom sink. I manage a little blue eyeliner, brush my teeth twice, gargle. An elastic-waist broomstick skirt goes down to my ankles and a black shirt that was bought form-fitting now hangs loose. One flat black shoe for the good foot. Silver stud earrings accent the steel of the crutches. My audience: The taxi driver for the half hour ride over the hill to the Valley, a roulette of hospital receptionists, nurse Carryl and orthopedic technician Bernie, Dr. Mesna and the x-ray staff. The office for *Men's Fitness* magazine isn't far from the hospital, so my friend Mike says he'll swing by to give me a lift home and save me the $65 cab fare. I promise him that one day I'll be able to drive Matt's truck, it's an automatic, no clutch, and I will quit asking for the favor. "No rush," he says. "That's just what L.A. needs. Another woman on painkillers behind the wheel."

I complain loudly about the doctor visits but, really, I have come to love being here. I am encouraged to go into detail describing my pain, how I am learning to move on crutches, talk of swelling, any signs of fever. There is much analyzing, worried hemming and hawing over x-rays, the doctor slowly examining the wound for signs of infection and slow healing. Dr. Mesna sometimes brings in colleagues to examine my situation so they can confer on treatment. I feel strangely relieved by the concern. The evidence proves the stakes are high, it is not just my imagination.

The trip from the curb to the lobby feels epic, through the Strait of Messina, past the rock of Cyclops. The cumbersome arrangement of my crutches; lifting my body out of the cab seat; the matter of my purse, how to carry it; the curb that looks like a cliff; doors, God, doors; the ever-present possibility of slipping or being bumped and falling, anticipating what degree of pain that would cause. Five minutes and already inside the black shirt my skin is damp with sweat. But when I reach the reception desk, I know I'm safe, finally to Ithaca. Carryl comes out quickly to fetch me from the waiting area.

"Sam! Get in here," she barks, waving me in. This affection from her warms my heart. Smoker's skin, the New York edge of her voice that resists being dulled by years of Southern California living. Carryl has seven kids, two ex-husbands and she is surprised by exactly nothing.

I am not on the examination table more than two minutes before she attacks the dressing on the wound with scissors. "Yuck," she says when the scissors have cut through all the bandages. The black cross-stitch is gone but the skin up and down the leg is still a kaleidoscope of purple and yellow, thick scabs at the break with a dark ooze and swelling all over. "You look like the Bride of Frankenstein." This is a kind of honor, being on the receiving end of the humor the medical staff reserve only for those they think can hack it.

"I heard that line before. You got it from *Full Metal Jacket*." The key to playing along is to just pretend to be my mother. The two of them would be good friends.

Bernie has come to set the new dressing and hears our exchange. A gold chain dresses up the v-neck of his blue smock, an earring in the shape of a lightning bolt shines on one lobe. "What do you expect?" he tells Carryl. "This is basically a reattached limb."

Bernie loosens the wraps of the splint, whistles. "Oh baby, you are so *hot!*" he points to the wiry hairs that spring from the skin, now a good inch long. They create the illusion of a burnt forest after a fire. "When are you going to shave? Please? For me?"

"How can I shave something I can't feel and can't get wet?" I am trying for a hip, ironic tone but my voice has developed a chronic flinch to it, a sort of yelping pitch.

"Never mind," he says. "I'm getting you a Norelco for Christmas."

Today for Show and Tell, Dr. Mesna brings with him another patient, a man in a walking cast up to his knee, leaning on a cane in an expert way that makes it clear he's walked like this for a while. Dr. Mesna introduces us, says we have something in common: legs snapped by horses. The man's bones haven't knitted after more than a year, although the injury is only a Grade II, B fracture, meaning the bones didn't even break the skin. No soft tissue damage. Not nearly as severe as my injury.

Amateur.

Dr. Mesna directs the man closer to the lighted wall where my X-rays hang. "See," he says to the man, pointing to the picture of the metal rod filling the center of the damaged bone, the screws attaching just below the knee, other screws just above the ankle joint, their ends poking through the sides. "This is the type of internal fixation device I was telling you about. There are a number of benefits—"

"No way!" the man doesn't even let Dr. Mesna finish the sentence. "That thing looks so nasty. I would never want anything so ugly."

I just look at him, mouth gaping. Does he realize I, the person on the table next to him, am the person to whom those x-rays belong? That by his saying out loud this astoundingly stupid and illogical comment I will feel so worthless, damaged beyond repair? Forget external appearances, the messy core of me has been judged ugly. I think of Gram, who put lipstick on even to garden, even in a garden inside the chain-link fence that bound the trailer lot in Las Vegas. *Never know who you're going to meet.*

Dr. Mesna is, as usual, unflappable, his reaction positively

Vulcan. "You understand, of course, that were are looking at an x-ray. The fixator is internal, it can't be seen. The nonunion of your fracture suggests this might be an acceptable course of treatment."

"I've seen all I need to," the man says. As he turns his back to leave Carryl catches my eye and looks heavenward, mouths the word "jerk." I once would have strode after him, ready to duke it out, yelling, "Did your horse step on your head too or have you always been an ignorant motherfucker?" But now anger dissipates as quickly as it gathers.

Dr. Mesna seems not to have noticed anything disagreeable just occurred. If I said something to him like, Why did you bring that moron in here?, he would be sincerely befuddled, he would never want to hurt my feelings, he simply is unsure how all this subjective stuff operates. I can imagine this particular quality of his, this earnest oblivion, makes his wife want to throw things at him.

"Ms. Dunn." He turns his attention to me. The tissue healing on the wound is "acceptable," he says. "Not great, but that's what you would expect of this kind of injury." I feel embarrassed, like this was a test I should have aced but instead squeaked by with only a C-. I'll have a surgery next week because he needs to take out the screws by my knee; the bone eventually will slide down the rod toward the break, helping to spur some growth. A Popsicle melting along a stick. "And you've got to start walking for a little bit every day with your crutches, putting as much pressure on the leg as you can stand. Weight-bearing activity is the only hope of creating bone."

I look at him blankly. All I can picture is the sight of that leg cut half open, angled to the side of my body, the attachment of muscle and sinew the only connection holding it to the rest of me. I want to tell him, Listen, you don't understand. I'm an invalid. We invalids don't do things like that. Invalids stay in bed. We sleep. We avoid touching our attached legs. We avoid having anything or anybody else touch it, either.

"Oh. Joy." My smile is anemic.

■ ■ ■

I arrive home to find a message from Drew on the answering machine. No luck leasing Harley. "One woman seemed interested but she backed out," he says. "Let me know and I'll keep trying."

The woman phoned me just last week; she'd given Harley a test ride and found him stiff, and tight on the left side. She wasn't impressed, still, she would like to start riding again. Why, exactly, was I laid up? "He jumped on me, and cut my leg half off," I explained, "but he didn't mean to." Her stumbling reply was the tip off she wouldn't be calling back.

I know I sabotaged the deal. But it's as if by leasing Harley I will lose who I am. Who I really am. Or at least was.

But the first of the month isn't far away. My half of the rent I should make good on. Board must be paid, all the bills of horseshoeing and vetting must be met, and then there is the expense of having the trainer Calvin MacDonald, the man I took weekly lessons with before the accident, exercise Harley to keep him healthy. Harley has arthritis from old racing injuries, he needs work to keep his joints supple. Matt even found this basement apartment in Malibu just so we could remain near the stable; there are cheaper places than this by far in Los Angeles. I should just release the idea of having a horse. Find Harley a cheap pasture somewhere in another county, maybe donate him to a riding program.

Yes. Pasture makes the most sense. The horse will be fine. Who am I kidding? I won't ride again. Owning a horse is completely anachronistic, I know this.

Instead, I pick up the phone and call one of my former editors at *Shape* magazine. She's surprised to hear from me, wants to know how I'm doing. Feeling great. Yeah, much better. "Hey, guess what," I say, "I'm up for assignments."

She is quiet on the other end of the line, then, with all delicacy, asks what I feel I can do.

"How about a hiking trip in Costa Rica?"

But there is no laughter on the other end.

I give up. "Seriously, I have an idea. I've been doing a little research on the idea of what makes people accident-prone."

At the turn of the twentieth century, industrial accidents were a common problem which cost plant owners time and money, so a number of studies were done investigating how to lower accident rates. What researchers found were: one, that people who have had accidents were more likely to have another than those who had not, and, two, that a few people in any one plant were the ones who suffered the majority of the accidents. British researchers Farmer and Chambers were the first to use the label "accident prone" in 1926. The seeds of why such a label might be important were planted some seventy years earlier, when a Massachusetts Supreme Court judge introduced the idea of personal negligence into legal liability. Before that, victims were rewarded without questions of over whether their actions had contributed in any way to the accident. But industrialization made it economically important to assign blame.

Studies tried to identify which factors might make some people more likely to experience accidents than others. Unequal exposure to hazards explained a few—the law of averages says a guy whose job it is to use a slicing machine is more likely to get cut than the boss who sits behind a desk. Differing levels of skill and training explained others. And, finally, it was determined that a person's state of mind was a more temporal factor, but nevertheless significant. Simply put: Hotheads who are reckless and don't pay attention get hurt. So do people who are preoccupied, or under stress.

Sigmund Freud was particularly intrigued by what seemingly chance occurrences, gaffes and accidental injury expressed about the subconscious. In *The Psychopathology of Everyday Life*, published in 1899, Freud said that "certain shortcomings in our psychical functioning and certain seemingly unintentional performances" all have motives "unknown to consciousness." Accidents were to him expressions of unconscious intent, and the more severe the accident, the more it expressed a desire for self-destruction.

Child psychology, sports medicine, emergency medicine, and psychiatry are just a few of the categories under which the subject of accident proneness has subsequently been examined, although on something of a hit-or-miss basis. The concept is "frequently discussed and rarely documented," researchers in the journal *Pediatrics* noted. Some still reject the notion entirely, saying there's no statistical measure for accident proneness, that it serves as a convenient way to "blame the victim." Arguments against the notion are most commonly put forward in cases of industrial accidents—ironically where the need to define the accident prone began—because it is used as a way to obscure the issue of companies putting people to work in potentially unsafe environments.

But in the available research from the vast array of disciplines that have, at some point or other, tried to identify why some people suffer accident after accident, one phrase keeps being repeated: "psychological factors."

Many times studies begin with the baseline-personality-type-that-just-takes-more-risks premise. By the law of averages, these personalities will get hurt more often as a result. But no matter the starting point, researchers inevitably get around to suggesting that some kind of psychological problem is lurking. An unconscious form of hurting yourself as a form of punishment for deep feelings of guilt. A misguided expression of grief. Even a self-defeating strategy to avoid dealing with success.

Or, in the language of research abstracts: "...Victims of trauma, both unintentional and especially intentional, have a high incidence of psychopathology," the *Journal of Trauma* noted, listing depression among the factors. *Clinical Orthopedics* observed that "vulnerability [to accidents] involves both physical and psychological faculties... the condition is referred to as 'accident proneness' especially when vulnerability is affected by psychologic predisposition." When depression in children is expressed through activity psychologists use the term *depressive equivalent.* In adults the same idea is called "agitated depression," where syndromes like low self-esteem are manifested in behavior.

Even when the researchers don't use any term that begins with the prefix "psycho," they still refer to influences on mental health, as in this study from *Pediatrics*: "children undergoing stressful changes in their lives were more susceptible to accidents..."

Most studies appear to look only at male subjects or mixed groups, rather than females. One study of trauma victims did note that while heavy drinking, aggression and other "conduct problems" were clear precursors to accidents experienced by men, for women those indicators were "less accurate." At one point a group within the American Psychiatric Association lobbied for a diagnosis called masochistic character disorder, but other argued against it, saying the potential for the label to be applied to women more than men invited discrimination.

But then there is this: in 1994, psychologist Dusty Miller published a book titled *Women Who Hurt Themselves.* In it she proposes that women who hurt themselves—whether through cutting, burning, being bulimic or anorexic, compulsively seeking plastic surgery or through substance abuse—suffer from what she calls "Trauma Reenactment Syndrome." Miller observes that, without exception, these women come from backgrounds that were either abusive or abnormally stressful in some other regard: "Her behavior is... a cry for help, a request for the protection she did not receive as a child." She believes these women use their bodies in essence to reenact the harm done to them as children, because there is a strange comfort in it, and because it reinforces some deeply imbedded belief that they are incapable of protecting themselves because they could not protect themselves as children. She doesn't talk about accidents per se as a way of hurting yourself, but her theories seem to echo larger themes in other studies that do.

■ ■ ■

I tell myself: In the last hundred years most of the rest of Freud's theories have been dismissed, better literature than science. As for the rest, they might as well be pot shots in the dark. Not one expert knows anything for sure.

So why then does it feel as if a wall is falling on my head, me in bed buried in the rubble of things said and unsaid during thirty-two years. I turn off the computer. I shut my eyes. My jigsaw memories.

■ ■ ■

Gram's face in front of me, *Sure, I'll take another highball,* holding out her glass, which had a hunting picture of pheasants being flushed out of the brush etched around the sides. *Whoopsie daisy!* she'd say if and when any Scotch was spilt. It would run down her arm onto the gold fabric of the Laz-E Boy. She always wore a short string of white plastic pearls around her neck, the plastic glowing with an unhealthy luminance, a certain larval quality. There Mom would be, leaning on the arm rest of the davenport, her stocking feet tucked under her, a practice that eventually eroded the fabric off the cushion, a permanent imprint worn into the foam. Re-reading one of the paperbacks she bought at Safeway, her head bowed toward the pages while my grandmother recited the chronology of my mother's failures. Gram had a lovely voice if you didn't listen to what she was actually saying. I knew Mom was memorizing the plot lines and historical facts from James Michener, from Irving Stone, as if they could replace what was being put in her head. And if that didn't work, she would drink more. It never worked.

Some people will pay big money to see what happens when a wolverine and a bear are chained together and thrown into a pit. I can say for sure that one will die and one will come out scarred and limping.

To be the chain that links the two.

Gram's face turned from me. *I'll marry whoever I want.* She had the rose clippers in her right hand. The seventy-year-old flesh of her arms jiggled as she trimmed the branch. *Whomever. I am sure you will.* Snap, snap. *Oh, fuck you.* She stopped for a minute but still didn't turn to me. *Well fuck you too, you little bitch.* But her voice wavered. Mine had not. I had mastered her art and she knew it. I walked out the gate to my car. She called to me. I didn't turn around.

Three weeks before the wedding. *Evelyn had a massive stroke. She was dead before the ambulance got here, Sammy.* Mom always called her mother by her first name. I had not telephoned since the day of the roses. I went home to New Mexico; Las Cruces, six hours farther south of where I was reared. Mom and I cleaned out her mobile home, "manufactured housing" is the current term, now in an upscale park with a guard at the gate, a swimming pool and club house, blue collar bourgeoisie. Emptied generic gin bottles insulated all the cupboards in the kitchen. The Funk & Wagnalls dictionary by the Laz-E Boy, its broken spine splinted by duck tape, pages soft from use, the ink down some columns smeared where she had run her index finger repeatedly, as if the tip could absorb all the words. Her last crossword, done in ballpoint. In the bedroom, the sewing box was opened. She had been making me a veil for the wedding. Mexican lace. I didn't wear it.

And why am I thinking of Gabe, the speckled pink and gray skin around his eyes, the dense white lashes. Boarded at a ranch when I went to Australia my senior year of high school. I feed him carrots in the pasture before I went to college. He was sold to pay for back board; by then Mom had taken a job in the Middle East and would be gone for nine years. Mom said it was Gram's fault and Gram said it was Mom's fault but I knew it was really my fault. A kid's camp bought him, the rancher said. Nice people, right up here off the highway, don't worry, he'll be happy. The rancher gave me the number. I kept it in my purse and I never again saw the animal that lifted me through my childhood.

But only when I think of the past two years do the tears become sobs, my ribcage growing sore from the heaving. People will say, *After the time alone, the meals she never made, the times she was never there, the times he was never there, the band practices, the drugs, the horse, the money she spent, all that money, and the amplifiers in black boxes, and the guitar strings, and the guitar picks called Fender Mediums he leaves in his jeans and how they always end up clanking around in the washer. And then the rehab and the therapy and the group sharing for the families of addicts and the steps she refused to take, sitting in the back of those meeting halls, glaring at her fellow participants and thinking, "This is his problem, not mine" and "I will not come to believe you were powerless, just take responsibility for your complete fuckup" and Losers, losers, whiners, losers.*

■ ■ ■

How long do I stay like this. Hours. The sun burns out over the ocean, night seeps into the room. Matt arrives home, a clatter in the kitchen. "I love you," he says when he comes into the room. "Do you want something to eat?" No. He leaves a minute later to watch TV in the living room, likely to fall asleep on the couch again. The bedroom becoming my exclusive kingdom, no way for him to get comfortable on this bed with all the pillows and me who cries out in pain at any unintentional nudge.

I flip the light switch by the bed and turn the computer back on.

■ ■ ■

In 1945, the American psychoanalyst Helen Flanders Dunbar put forth the description of the accident prone as those who are drawn to adventure and excitement, in search of immediate pleasure. This type of person does not like to plan ahead and detests discipline of any form, including the self-discipline it takes to exercise caution. But Dunbar is most famous for adding the term "psychosomatic" to the popular vernacular; she argued that all illness must be looked at in the context of a person's life, because psychology and biology fit hand and glove. She saw the symptoms of any one illness as being "insight symbols," potentially revealing why at a particular time in life a person is suffering a particular ailment or—she notes this specifically—accident in the case of fracture patients.

Accident as allegory. For Flanders, like Freud, there was always a mystery to unravel behind any accident. Sometimes a broken leg is a cigar.

■ ■ ■

For the next several days I sift through the research abstracts, books and essays I have accumulated, mentally constructing the story of my life, what led to the final climax where I decide to get off my horse and cross the stream. What motivates the main character? This: because she was born the illegitimate child of a single mother who was struggling through night school to earn a college degree, she felt she was the reason her mother had been forced to live with her grandmother in a miserable alliance to rear her. Later, she was the reason her stepfather died because she had failed to find the experimental drugs in Mexico her mother gave her money to buy. Finally, she was such a horrible wife that her husband became an addict to escape the reality of their hollow life together, and she didn't stop him. She keeps hurting herself in a subconscious effort to atone for it all, breaking her leg as a symbol of saying, I can't run from this anymore.

Or, to nab attention for herself away from the recovering husband.

The plot is complex, her motives are never pure.

■ ■ ■

It is just after Thanksgiving when I return home from the hospital after my surgery to remove the screws near the knee. I don't dare venture beyond the circuit of the bed to the couch to the bathroom. Dr. Mesna says I have to walk, but I reason that by limiting all motion I can cut to nil the odds of me having an accident.

I explain that my lack of movement is owed to pain, but there is always some degree of pain, not a minute I've been without it since the instant Harley's hoof cut through the shin. The truth is I feel as if I have a bomb strapped to my chest, I could go off at any time. Any misstep, any spilt glass, a book dropped to the floor, evidence of my psychopathology.

■ ■ ■

Edward listens for some minutes while I confess all this to him, the receiver made slick from the perspiration of my cheek. I never know when he is going to call, I just pick up the phone and there he is, voice calm, there is never any small talk, sometimes not even a hello, he is way beyond grades, like a personal Obi-Wan Kenobi.

Finally he interrupts. "This is the problem of psychoanalyzing yourself," he says. Some of this may be true, sometimes. Some of it may not be. Some of it is crap you can completely discount. He says I am missing the point.

I feel as if he's just deliberately ripped off my shell, which took me so long to find and fit myself into like a hermit crab. Edward has never talked to me like this.

"The question is, what are you going to do about your life now?" he asks. "I remember seeing you in the dirt, and the look in your eye. I said to myself, This has the reek of karma all over it. It was literally a breaking point. You could go one way or the other."

Karma, the accumulation of choices and action. Not like kismet, the Turkish concept of fate or fortune, beyond measure and calculation. I want directions, right or left? But he isn't offering, says I'm the only one who can figure it out. This is the old struggle, the big question, trying to construct meaning out of what we cannot know, because to do otherwise would mean one of two things, either that existence is random, or that the design is more profound than we can fathom. "What we are really talking about is faith," he says. "Do you have it?"

Faith, a noun, meaning confident trust in a person, idea or thing. "Sometimes," I say. "It depends."

It sometimes crosses my mind that I am not having these conversations with him at all, that this is a figment played out in my head. I make him tell me the story of my rescue in some shape or form, as if it's a bedtime story. Each time he calls he reveals a new detail so I know it's real. Today I begin with, "I remember you kept pushing my hair back. I could tell you didn't want me to look."

"I had to lean over you," he says. "The only way I could get the bleeding to stop was by pinching the artery shut with my fingers."

I have a slightly nauseous feeling, a jittery shake of muscle all at once, like the sensation of almost getting hit by a car but not quite. What did I think he was doing all that time kneeing over me? I look at my hand, I reach to touch my face, realizing this could be flesh dead and buried these months. I am too overwhelmed even to cry. The miracle of my life I owe to Edward and then to the paramedics, nurses, lab techs, doctors, all people who were willing to get their hands dirty. It occurs to me I have been operating my life on the fundamental lie that I am independent and making it on own. I exist because other people have stepped outside of what is comfortable for them and made it so.

"I didn't have a belt," he continues, "I couldn't think of anything for a tourniquet."

How much blood can you lose before you bleed to death? It happens quickly, that much I know. I recall a line from an article those years ago at *Emergency Medical Services Magazine*: Five liters in the average adult, about 70 ccs per kilogram of body weight.

I don't know what to say to him. I was not the only person experiencing stress and trauma that day of my accident.

I realize that canyon, next to his house, is a place he knows well. I wonder if the memory of literally holding a woman's life in his hands makes it a place he now wants to avoid. I ask, "Have you been back?"

"The next day," he says. The dried blood made a large brown circle where I lay, so he scrapped the dirt until it was cleared. "You never know. I thought it might scare people. Or if someone else came riding through there and the horse smelled it—something could happen again."

I try to imagine a circle large enough to scare a horse, the dull color, how fast blood will oxidize when exposed to air, a smell like something left in the refrigerator too long.

"Listen," he says, "what we were talking about before—don't get caught there, in the reasons why."

■ ■ ■

But that is exactly what I do, for days obsessively ferreting through computer link after link about accidents and the people who have them. I eat only peanut butter, toast and black tea, my mind too busy to make choices about food. Matt has learned to live on cafeteria food at the office and boxed cereal at home.

I find instructions for casting out demons—Pentecostals, God love them, upgrading from tents to cyber ministry. Accident proneness falls under a long list of "demon indicators," which include lying, wearing the color red, levitating, projectile vomiting, and using the Lord's name in vain. I think of the priest at my bedside in the hospital, the missed opportunity for exorcism. *The European Journal of Emergency Medicine* prints a study that proposes people who have repeated accidents have a higher rate of alcohol abuse and a "propensity towards violence." I report this to my mother. "They're just Irish," she says. I think of a black and white picture in her cedar chest of my Uncle Mutt, smiling, he looks like a fat George Clooney, in each fist a can of Colt 45, hunting cap on, rifle next to him, ready for deer season.

I am looking for the one oyster that holds the pearl, that one magic kiss or glass slipper. Once I have it I'll know that I have broken the spell, that I am not meant for accidental ruin, or at least that I have the power to choose against it.

The tendency to have accidents is not constant in my life, it arrives like a bad rash. This is supported by research. Some people are accident-prone for short periods, others suffer bouts their entire lives. People can be accident prone for different reasons at different periods in life, writes psychologist G.J.S. Wilde, Ph.D., author of *Target Risk*, one of the most comprehensive looks at the subject of risk factors yet compiled. Triggers that have been identified include problems in relationships, jobs and money matters, and loss of a loved one. *Rehab, freelancing, hospital bills, three out of four.* One study Wilde cites found that drivers suffering marital problems were more involved in accidents around the time they filed for divorce. That word again, divorce. Matt had said it on the phone in the first call from the hospital. No, I said. Then: If that's what you want. I didn't repeat the word. Like cancer. Don't say it too much or you bring it into being.

To believe accident proneness is a description of a person's nature is to commit what social psychologists call a "fundamental attribution error," meaning that a person's behavior is being held up as proof of his essential makeup or character, rather than being an indicator of his passing state of mind or environmental conditions. Get paid for it once and they'll always call you a whore, in other words.

The truth is I am not prone to accidents. I am prone to jumping on the back of a horse and riding until the rush of wind in my ears takes away the screaming and name calling between the two women I love most in the world. I am prone to going to the stable rather than asking my husband if he can please take that fucking bong out of his mouth. I am prone to panic over when I'm going to get paid for my last freelance article and whether the check will arrive before the phone bill is due. I am prone to fly off the handle. I am prone to be sad for reasons I don't really understand. I am prone to want to see myself bleed rather than say I'm scared. Accidents are just part of the deal.

"I'm thinking you might want to see your horse." Calvin MacDonald on the phone. A voice that booms from his barrel chest, he must stand six foot two, seems as big as some of the horses he rides, a self-titled Professional Irishman, bright blue eyes like gem stones out of place in a rough-hewn wood carving of a face.

"Is there something wrong?" The icy wash of guilt pours over me. For the past couple months I have literally turned my head as I pass the turn for the barn on the way to the medical center. I mail the board to Drew without even a note. Not willing to give Harley up but not willing to see him, either.

"No, no. I've been riding him." Calvin pauses for a moment. "But there's nothing like motherly love, now, is there? And it would do you good. Get some air in your lungs."

After we say goodbye I feel angry with Calvin. Doesn't he know how hard it is for me to get around? What does he expect? If I had my X-rays I would wear them like a necklace so no one would ever be confused and expect too much.

But then I start to wonder about particulars I have not considered since a time before that day on the trail. Harley is a hard keeper, prone to be skinny, he's bound to catch any sickness circulating in the barn. Have Drew and Juan, the groom, remembered to put wraps on Harley's front legs? He develops sores from the hard ground of his paddock without them. Has his mane been pulled? It grows so thick and unruly, black hair stronger than twine. It won't hurt to see him, I tell myself. Just to check. Be a responsible owner.

I take a Vicodin preventatively. My strategy for local travel is to take a pill, get in the car and drive to my destination, which is never more than ten minutes from the house. That way, I can drive before that slow-motion, numb feeling sets in. Once I get where I am going, walking around with my crutches and putting pressure on the leg every step or so will produce enough pain to wake me up again, so that by the time I have to drive back I'm just enough on edge to be alert. It occurs to me that this is exactly the kind of behavior those studies on the factors in accident proneness are talking about; I see researchers in lab coats pointing to a large Petri dish. *Exhibit A. Here we see the prototypical specimen.*

But what real choice do I have, to stay in the house for the next year, waiting for someone to take me out?

Well, yes.

Shut up.

■ ■ ■

The familiar stillness of late afternoon at the barn. Calvin is gone, no one around except Juan. The horses stand quietly, all with their heads down, noses rustling through their afternoon feeding, searching for the sweetest stalks of hay. I sweat going up the incline to Harley's paddock, sit on the mounting block next to the gate to catch my breath. He turns his head for a moment, then returns to his hay. I watch the play of his jaw muscles under his thin bay coat as he grinds the food with his teeth. The lids hang heavy over his eyes; he looks content, half asleep. His black tail swishes at the occasional fly. It nearly reaches the ground. I used to keep it trimmed and level but now the ends are jagged, like a bad haircut grown out.

Juan comes and sits beside me on the block. It is like him not to say hello, even after not having seen me for months. A baseball cap seems to be permanently attached to his head. He is not much more than a boy but has the polished, jet-stone eyes of a very old man.

"Sam." He says the "a" in my name in the soft way of

Spanish, not in the flat, nasal way of American English. He gestures up and down the length of my body. "You muy flaca now."

"I know. Pero es bien por una chica to be skinny, no es verdad?" We speak a kind of pidgin to each other, his English and my Spanish about on par. He thinks I should speak better Spanish because of where I grew up, I tell him he has to learn English to make money in the U.S. I remember we had been trying to improve each other's fluency, but neither one of us had ever seemed to improve much.

He looks down, pinching a stalk of hay in his fingers. "No, is no good. You have mucho dolor?"

"Si. I have pain todos los dias," I tell him.

"Es lastima," Juan says, shaking his head.

"You get used to it," I tell him. We sit for a moment not saying anything, and I remember how I used to be more at home here than in my own house, but now am uncomfortable, feel I am a part that no longer fits.

"I put Harley in el corral ahora," he says, motioning to the round pen where horses are lunged, and I reply yes, OK gracias. I poke my way slowly through the dirt as Juan takes Harley away from the hay and leads him to the pen. Juan closes the gate behind us and there we stand, Harley with his head down and me leaning on my crutches, not looking at each other, awkward, kids at a junior high dance. Finally I remember the carrot in my sweatshirt pocket I brought as an offering. His ears prick with mild interest. He starts to amble toward me with that loose walk of his and I have to steel myself from recoiling backwards, afraid, he so big and me so easily knocked down. But he stops beside me and nickers softly, not reaching for the carrot. He too seems a little skinnier, a little meeker.

"C'mon boy," I tell him, reaching out to run my hand across his neck. The hair is longer, slightly rougher than I recall. "Hey, do you remember our trick?"

Harley knows one stupid pet trick, the so-called camel stretch, a bow in which he stretches his head between his front hooves. He would grudgingly perform it for visitors only if I plied him with enough treats to make it worth his while. With the end of the carrot I cue him for the trick by tapping him on the side while holding onto my crutches. He blows air through his nostrils and bobs his head a couple of times. This is his oh-damn-she's-asking-me-to-do-that-thing response, unchanged in all these months, but then he surprises me by stretching down into a perfect bow.

"Guboy guboy guboy," I gush as I feed him the carrot, reverting to a cutesy voice I am prone to use around dogs and horses, when no human is within earshot. But Juan is used to catching me in the act, and this time, like all others, he just shakes his head and mouths the word "loca."

I start to feel light-headed from the sunshine, the Vicodin kicking in, and all the blood draining into the leg. "Juan," I say, my voice sounding feeble even to me, "necessito sit down. Can you open the gate por favor?" I pat Harley, then turn to make my way out of the pen, the dirt is deep and soft, makes for hard going. He follows behind me, puppy-like, and as I reach the gate he starts pawing the ground. I slowly turn, bracing myself, expecting him to frisk my pocket with his muzzle for evidence of more bounty. Instead he steps away, and without any prompting performs another bow. This is an obvious ploy for another carrot, but it makes me smile, and I realize I can't remember the last time I have really smiled other than to put on a happy face for Matt when he comes home.

"Sorry," I balance my weight against the crutches on my arm pits as I pull my hands away from the crutches to show him I'm not holding anything. "See? No more, you mooch." A bad move putting my weight on the crutches; the pressure slows the blood circulation in the arteries under the arms, making me feel even woozier. But again Harley paws the ground, and again, he bows. Praise again, then I turn on my crutches, but each of my movements produces a new bow, his hopeful look on each completion.

Tears run down my cheeks, I taste the salt of them on my

lips. "Whoa, whoa," I tell him, and he finally does, standing beside me. I steady myself against him, his warm coat on my cheek, and when he doesn't move I lean all my weight against him, propping my crutches on him and throwing an arm around his neck.

"Hey, Sam," says Juan, "you OK?"

"Si, si," I tell him, pressing my face into the groove where Harley's neck moves into his shoulder, as if I can draw all the strength from there. And I talk quietly to my horse as his head curves toward me, telling him a hundred things as his coat grows wet where I have buried my face. He stands very still.

My first social excursion: Meeting Renée for coffee at our local java bar in the overblown mini-mall that passes for Malibu's downtown. I drive the truck for the 10-mile trip, happy for the speed at which the roadside flashes by, appreciating the control of being behind a wheel, like I am sixteen again, driving all the way to Santa Fe in Gene's Mercury Comet.

But that sense of power evaporates the minute I manage to get myself out of the truck, my leg in a brace that encases the leg up to the knee and resembles the boots astronauts wore on the moon, crutches under both arms. My sweatshirt droops over my body, my shoulders like a wire hanger. In the parking lot cars drive past me, a truck whizzes so near I feel the rush of current on my face; I can easily see myself crushed under a wheel, I would make a popping sound not unlike an aluminum can. I try to hurry, I feel as if everyone is waiting for me to get the hell out of the way, and I think of the driving game Matt and I used to play, joking, Five points for the gimp! Ten if they're in a wheelchair, twenty for the blue hair shuffling in the walker. My punishment is not that I am the punchline of my own joke but that I keep hearing the aphorism *What comes around goes around* in my head to the tune of a song by Ratt. Retribution delivered by a heavy metal band; on which tier of Dante's seven-ring spiral am I, exactly?

In the window of the coffee shop I catch a glimpse of a woman plugging along crutches, her sharp cheekbones, the trench lines around her mouth, her back hunched as she grips the handles. I have a picture in my head of someone entirely different, a full-figured redhead with a stride designed to cover a lot of ground all at once. Not an urban, run-to-catch-a-cab walk, more of a steady rhythm developed tromping through pastures, on dirt roads. I cannot believe this the face and body the world now sees. How puny I am. I can see myself already an old woman, anxious of strangers, afraid of being hurt.

Renée has already staked out a table for us, she helps me situate my apparatus, arranges an extra chair for me to prop the leg on for elevation, too long down and it starts to swell and throb. I tell her I have seen Harley and begin to launch into the story of going back to the barn—she'll love this, I know, she has two cats and she knows how animals can be. She nods as I tell her, aw, that's sweet, really, but you weren't alone, were you?

"No," I reply, a little surprised, "Juan was there."

"Good." She looks relieved. "I think you should be careful." What she wants are the details of the appointments with Dr. Mesna, the most recent prognosis, descriptions of rehabilitation therapy. There are none to report. Dr. Mesna says there is nothing the hospital can do to grow bones that I can't do for myself, namely walk. And as for infection, beyond what they have already done in terms of aggressive antibiotic therapy, that's a throw of the dice. It will crop up later or it won't.

"I can't believe there's no rehab," she says. "Tell them you need better answers than that. Is it an HMO policy? I bet it is. I bet you it is."

As I listen to her I start to feel exhausted, and a little defensive. I trust my doctor. I need to trust my doctor. I don't have any energy to do anything but. I am an obedient patient. I tell her that's just the way it is with my injury. Best case scenario, I will always have a limp and swelling that will worsen as I age.

I must say this in more of a grandiose, self-pitying tone than I realize, because she replies sharply, "That's not so bad. There are worse things than a limp." I look at her in a way that means, That's easy for you to say, gorgeous Audrey Hepburn-looking creature, you who stops traffic, you who can drink cappuccino and elegantly avoid getting a foam moustache.

"You know, I have a limp." She throws this off matter-of-factly, and I am stunned. She nods and says yes, one leg is slightly shorter than the other, she wears s a small lift in one shoe. Have I never noticed?

Not in the almost-a-decade I have known her have I noticed this. I blush. To say that I am contrite doesn't reach far enough. I look at my dear friend and try to imagine that it is for the first time, trying to see the person who actually sits in front of me rather than the mirage of ideas and preconceptions I have put in her place. What else have I neglected?

"I am so sorry for being an asshole." I tell her reaching my hand out to touch her. Her wrist is so small. "I am really, truly sorry."

■ ■ ■

Renée leaves to run errands. Everyone lives within the lines determined, to one extent or other, by their physical abilities. Bodies change over time: everyone understands this is the process of age. How callow does it make me that this never occured to me before? Up to this point I contrived a life of perpetual motion, creating the illusion that life stays the same. But when such constant movement isn't possible, now that that I have watched the hands on a clock move forward from seconds to minutes to hours, I am beginning to appreciate the reality of change. I feel a profound sense of shame for the cocoon that I have built of my suffering, savoring what I silently believed to be its singularity.

"Skiing accident?" An older man in a polo shirt and tan slacks comes up to me as I sit on a bench near a granite fountain at the mini-mall outside of a flower shop.

"Horse," I say.

"I had a bad fall on skis once," he crosses his arms and stands beside me for a moment, commiserating on the healing process. "Well, get better," he finally says and with a wave he turns in the direction of the coffee shop.

When I could walk I never spoke to anyone in public places like this. No one ever said hello, I never said hello. But now I notice if I shut up and listen, people talk to me in a way they never have. Because my injury is so obvious and my movement labored, I am easy to catch. Some people look away when they see me, as if made uncomfortable by my crutches and brace, but then I realize many more look directly at me, often stopping to say offer encouragement or even talk. And when they speak, it's not for idle chatter. *I lost my bladder to cancer, I have a bag that attaches. I am so depressed. I was on crutches for a bad sprain, it still hurts. My daughter died horseback riding. My ankle had to be pinned in five places when a motorcycle ran over it.* They show me the missing parts of fingers lost in freak fishing mishaps, the lines of scars that pull at skin like ragged hems, the hearing aides behind the careful arrangement of hair. This was not part of my landscape before.

I run my hand over the rough stone of the bench and think about the people I have professed to love. How terrified Matt must have been that first night in the drug treatment center, unfamiliar bed and strange faces around him. My mom, how she had cried in pain and frustration those years ago when she cut her hand trying to jimmy loose a bad muffler on our old car with a piece of rusty bailing wire. A friend who works as a newspaper reporter, learning her lovely brown Cleopatra eyes are betraying her with macular degeneration. My grandmother, shutting her eyes against the stab of a migraine, saying how much she hated rainy days, remembering being a child looking up at the stars to see if she could find the face of her dead mother, and how she would talk to the stars and wait for them to break their silence. How eventually she stopped looking up all together. The shotgun metal, the last taste my uncle knew as he decided how to die.

I make a vow to hold these pictures in my mind, fragile, some beautiful crystal image easily crushed. Then, instantly, I feel sad. It is my nature to forget vows.

■ ■ ■

My phone has started to ring off the hook with calls from my old stable of magazine editors who now want to know if I'm up for an assignment. Small assignments, mostly, brief blurbs of information I can easily track down by phone. I suspect something is going on but I don't want to ask too many questions, lest I jinx the current boon and have the phone go silent again. They never called this often when I had two good legs. Journalists are by nature inclined to collect and pass information amongst each other, and that includes any gossip on one of their own. The news on me makes good copy: *Maimed by her horse! She and her husband had been on the rocks, are they together? How is she going to make it?* They have been trading worried clucks, flipping through the stacks of papers on their desks for items they can give me to work on from my laptop desk in bed. I am grateful; it's given me a way to measure days, a reason to look at the calendar apart from the one day I go to the doctor.

The most frequent caller is Stephanie, my editor at *InStyle* who has become a solid Grade 1, calling for regular updates, wanting to know about my injury in photographic detail. She knows about the shiny scar that runs jagged and twisted around the circumference of my shin and the dent in my calf muscle, the vertical mark from the bolt placement on the inside of my ankle, another on the outside of my calf, and still another that looks like a centipede running down my knee. "Sam-a-lama," she always says by way of hello, "want to make some money, honey?"

The assignment this week is to simply compile a list for a "fitness trends of the stars" piece on yoga and martial arts teachers who have celebrity clients. So far this has been easy for me to track down: After years writing about health and fitness I have a Rolodex full of names, and celebrities in Los Angeles are like ragweed in the rest of the country—you can't drive down the road without seeing some. In another sense, though, it has reminded me of all that I cannot do, and will likely never be capable of again. I conduct all the interviews over the phone, keeping them brief, just the facts ma'am, politely declining the offers to come try out a class, come see the great gym.

A friend at *Shape* gives me a lead for a yogi named Gurmukh Kaur Khalsa. Grrr-MOO-k, I take the name down phonetically. A teacher of Kundalini yoga, whatever that is, a list of famous names longer than my arm is said to attend the classes. I roll my eyes. *L.A., land of fruits and nuts*, Mom often tells me. She reads the magazines at the supermarket, she's far more current in the Hollywood gossip than I am. *Just don't join a cult, for chrissakes.*

I call. A small voice answers on the other end, "Sat nam, Hello?" stringing the sounds together so they become one word, satnamhellooo? I have the urge to say, Is your mommy home, Satnam?, but instead I ask for Grrr-MOO-k.

"This is she," replies the voice, and for a moment I don't know what to say. I was expected an old Indian man with a thick accent. I tell her who I am and what I'm doing, can I get some information please on her classes.

"I would love to tell you all you need," she says, "Why don't you come down here?"

"I just have a few quick questions—"

"It's just that I hate to talk over the phone. It's so much better if I can show you." she replies. "I like to have a face to go with a name."

This woman clearly is not going to budge; contact with celebrity is a kind of celebrity in itself, many in this town have figured that out and have learned to leverage the most mundane things for the optimal amount of publicity. This person is probably no exception. I consider ringing off with a "Sorry to have bothered you" but I don't. There is something quaint about this woman who talks like Glinda, the good witch of the north. She asks if I can be at her house in an hour, and I want to tell her to expect something damaged, that I have not been farther than the coffee shop in six months, that I walk with the aid of a leg brace and crutches, that despite the Vicodin I take every six hours I feel ground down by the aches that grate along my nerves, and that I am perpetually exhausted regardless of the fact I sleep fourteen hours a day. I am just too tired to argue with Glinda. I get dressed; my clothes hang on me like laundry on a line. I drive the forty minutes to her house, as directed. It is surprisingly easy to meld with the traffic on the freeway. Mike was right. Just another woman on painkillers.

■ ■ ■

The house is a Hollywood bungalow, tile roof, stucco walls, pampas grass overgrown and an uneven path leading from the yard to the door. I bite my lip as I plod along the path, certain I will fall, wondering what the hell I was thinking to say yes to a yoga teacher, Birkenstock-wearing-Volkswagen-driving-tofu-eating-noodle-neck who spoon-feeds New Age hoopla to TV actresses. I am so angry by the time I reach her patio entrance I have to catch my breath.

Each inhale is perfumed with the scent of the jasmine vines running along the walls, and *nag champa* wafts through the open windows into the courtyard. I know incense, how you burn it to get rid of the skunky residue of marijuana, but this smell doesn't have the scent of hiding anything. A little plug-in fountain for good feng shui gurgles by the carved wood door, purple geode crystals line the sides of the steps, a strategy to attract positive vibrations. You can't grow up around Santa Fe without at some point being immersed in the culture of the New Age—and, sure enough, a New Mexico flag, its bright yellow background and red Zia sun symbol, decorates a wall by the window. The collective impression is so goofy I find myself laughing out loud. A four-foot statue of a grinning elephant god only makes me laugh harder. Silly Ganesha, Hindu god of auspicious beginnings.

The door opens and a slight, barefoot woman dressed all in white says hello, sizing me up with a quick look over my body. On her head is a white turban held at the center by a topaz the size of a baby's fist. Behind her others in white turbans and Indian dress walk by, looking like some ward in a celestial version of the Red Cross. I relax. I know the deal here, they're American Sikhs, hippies who found a guru and got clean, they run a huge ashram in northern New Mexico, used to operate a health food restaurant on the Santa Fe Plaza where as a junior high kid I'd scam cookies. I have a rush of nostalgia, it is a warm feeling.

"Oh, wow. What happened to you?" Gurmukh doesn't introduce herself. "Here, come in. Let's sit on my bed so you can put your feet up and have some tea." She leads me down a hall past beaded curtains to a room of rococo design and cozy opulence. Oriental carpets warm the wood floors, a double bed covered in pale-shaded pillows fills a corner. By comparison I have a sense of being awkward, too severe, my black turtleneck and wide-leg pants stiff and uncomfortable.

We sit for nearly two hours on her bed. I am the one supposed to be doing the interviewing but she asks all the questions, my life strung out. As she listens she just nods, sometimes shutting her eyes, expressing no pity for me, not even a "that must have hurt." I feel glad about that. While I have come to expect attention because of my injury, the price of that attention is pity, its insidious effect a feeling of hopelessness, as if my very essence as a person has been reduced.

Then it is her turn to talk, and she becomes a Scheherazade spinning story after story, about her previous life as a flower child in Haight Ashbury, how she'd stumbled onto life as a yogini, tales about washing the floors in golden temples in India. She is the kind of person who says the word "God" with no question mark at the end. She tells me to return tomorrow to take her yoga class. I laugh because I think she's trying to be funny.

"You can get well," she says, like to Dorothy about the red slippers. "You just need to decide you're going to."

My guard goes up; I have been lulled by this fairy-looking hippie who is now going to tell me my pain is all in my head and to drink wheatgrass. I look at her like she is crazy, if she tells me my broken leg is in my head I'll snarl at her.

She sees my look and waves it off. "People in wheelchairs can do Kundalini yoga," she says in a way that makes it sound practical, like taking out the trash or doing the dishes. "Even if you only sit there and breathe for three minutes, those three minutes will help you. We always say, Begin where you are."

I tell her I'll think about it and then I return to the car. For several minutes after I put the key in the ignition, I sit staring out the windshield at the city street. It is January of the year I will be thirty-three years old. My hands grip the steering wheel, and for some reason I start to cry, really cry, the asphalt of the street and the row of stucco homes in front of me growing blurry, my sobs loud enough for an old woman wheeling a grocery cart on the sidewalk to turn and look at the truck. It's if I have been wandering in the rain for a long time, and have stumbled onto some shelter. I am afraid to go in, but also afraid to stay out in the rain.

■ ■ ■

I surprise myself by actually showing up to the yoga class. The problem had been what to wear, pawing through my few remaining clothes in the chest of drawers, finally giving up and putting on pajama bottoms. At her house I position myself at the back of the wood-floored living room she uses as a yoga studio, crutches against the wall. A smiling woman with long blond hair helps me sit on the floor, the leg in its brace stretched out in front. This is the first time I have been on a floor since my accident, and it makes me think of the canyon dirt, how exposed I am, and suddenly I am scared. I feel like hell. I look like hell. What am I doing here with these granolas?

Gurmukh comes in, the woman in her late fifties with the gait of a teenager. She waves at me, says she's glad I made it. The others in class turn to look at me and I put my head down, feeling like a child, if I don't look at them maybe they'll go away.

To begin the class she has us put our hands together, thumbs pressed to the center of the chest, and close our eyes. "We always begin with a chant," she explains. "These ancient and sacred sounds mean that we are bowing to the great infinite wisdom found inside ourselves." I listen to the others as Gurmukh leads them in flat Sanskrit tones, *Ong Namo Guru Dev Namo*, and in my head are images of the Muslim call to prayer, the summer I spent in Saudi Arabia with my mother while she worked there, every person on their knees, the plaintive pitch of such strange words as they echoed over the barren sky. It strikes me that I have not prayed with my hands together since I was a child, even in church those occasional times I was too proud or self-conscious to do more than bow my head. Now I push my thumbs tighter against my chest as if to pry loose something stuck there and feel for the first time in my life the urge to pray, speak in tongues, howl and let the sound fall on whatever is there, if anything is there.

We inhale the word *Sat*, exhale the word *Nam*, which, she explains, when said together mean "truth is my identity"; Sikhs use it as hello and goodbye. I consider what it can mean if truth is my identity. If that is always so, then my relationship to every other definition I have used for myself changes, so that they are like clouds, or a morning fog, transient by nature. Accident-prone. Invalid. Wife. Even daughter.

When the class moves to standing postures Gurmukh directs me to sit and breathe, holding the positions in my mind. What we are doing, she says, is raising the Kundalini, the very energy of life. It sits coiled in the base of our spines, the movements like the flute of the snake charmer to the cobra, moving it up our spines to awaken us. I shut my eyes and listen to every word she says. The last posture is to lay flat out on our backs, feel rolled out. She says it is called corpse pose, and I think of lying in the dirt again, Edward's fingers dyed crimson. I feel a touch and I open my eyes to see Gurmukh standing over me, turning my palms up toward the ceiling. "If you keep your hands closed, how will you receive your blessings from God?"

she says matter-of-fact.

In that class I experience a sensation that is not unlike falling in love.

■ ■ ■

That night I dream of snakes coiling around my spine, their eyes of topaz and moonstone, so many of them, until I myself become them. I see again the flying V of Harley's stomach, but this time I am quick and supple, no appendages to hit. I hear with my body the vibrations of his hooves as they land then gallop away, fading as thunder does when a storm rolls out to the ocean.

I am at Gurmukh's classes three days a week, four if I don't sleep late on Saturdays. I would stay at her house if I could. I observe the way the yogis live, take any suggestion as an order; this is the way I learn foreign languages, mimicking every detail until I become fluent. As my yoga teacher does, so do I. Like her, I take now cold showers each morning, waking up as Matt leaves for the long commute to work. The process begins by massaging almond oil into my skin, all my skin, including the skin of the leg, where I can feel the sensation of pressure but not touch. It is difficult for me to do the first time. I love my hand over my knee, the centipede scar, how white and shiny, then lower, to near the break. I have this fear that if I touch it too hard it will snap right off, like a dead branch on a tree. There is an indentation in the shin where the hoof penetrated and a sharp curve at the back where the muscles and shin were sewn together. Otherwise there is nothing but an uneven line around my calf, the mark like the serrated edge of a blade.

At first the sensation of touching the part of the leg below the break is like holding a steak before you put it on the grill, fleshy, heavy. But by the end of the week this part of my body starts to feel familiar again, there's a section of my calf that seems almost normal, my foot has feeling although my toes are stiff. My ribs I count like keys on a xylophone. Then under the cold needles of water I scrub until every inch of me is rosy, the cold making the chunk of metal in my leg hum, like striking a tuning fork. But, after, my skin feels warm from all the blood brought to the surface.

After I dry off, I go into the bedroom to meditate for half an hour, rolling the still-foreign chants on my tongue. I thought meditating would be easy—I have spent months in bed, after all, how much more immobile can you get—but at first I twitch and am antsy, five minutes passes slower than most hours I have lived. Then, I don't know when it happens or why on this day, but one morning I shut my eyes, open them, and 30 minutes has already gone by.

I eat a vegetarian diet—vegetables, fruit and even tofu, which I have difficulty figuring out how to cook, because every concoction I manage has an unappealing non-taste.

My days are increasingly filled with the business of healing, putting me on the road for a forty-mile round trip in Matt's truck. I see a Sikh chiropractor who manipulates the toes of my bad leg and cracks my neck, a Korean acupuncturist who pokes bamboo in me the size of hat pins and burns a strange moss on my skin like incense. The theory of the moss burning I don't really follow, but it's supposed to put the body's immune system into a kind of overdrive, and I drink hot milk flavored with turmeric and honey, because the yogis swear it's good for bones—not because of the calcium in milk, but because turmeric is said to have certain healing powers. It tastes like chalk. I don't ask questions. I willingly enter the Province of Suspension of Disbelief, which no one in my life wants to follow me into.

"You're a *vegetarian* now?" Tina asks incredulously when I call her, the way I imagine she would if I were to announce I was actually a transsexual, or a Republican. "You can't be a vegetarian. You're a real New Mexican, not a hippie New Mexican. How do you suppose we make vegetarian carne asada? We don't, pendeja."

"Oh Christ," is my mother's response. "Is this like the time you joined Camp Fire Girls and I had to show up for those goddamn hikes in the woods?"

I am afraid Matt will pull out his twin sabers, wit and

sarcasm, and kill the pleasure I take from these new actions. He surprises me by remaining more or less detached and unbiased. It hits me that he is no longer the smart-ass guitar player who waltzed into that party years ago with the case of Schaefer light beer under his arm, but a man who has had to rethink much of what he believed about himself, more fragile around the edges, easily bruised. Well, not all smart-ass guitar player, at least.

"So if your yoga teacher told you to stand on your head and eat peanut butter sandwiches, you'd do it?" he wants to know when I tell him I'm forsaking sugar and artificial sweeteners in all their forms and will henceforth drink green tea instead of Coke.

"Of course." I answer without blinking.

"Well all righty then," he nods as he drinks his coffee, puts one hand up as if to say "I surrender."

Dr. Mesna proves less accepting, in fact the term "freaked out" best applies. Unwrapping my brace he sees prick patterns from acupuncture along the skin, red dots where the moss has been burned. "What, exactly, is going on here?" It seems that all the color has drained from his face, making his freckles appear larger.

I explain my recent enlightenment, how the acupuncture is stimulating my chi, the yoga unleashing my Kundalini, the chiropractic care aligning my body. "I am a healing machine," I tell him. I request that he make yoga a requirement for all his patients.

"Ms. Dunn, Ms. Dunn, Ms. Dunn." He rubs his eyes, puffs his cheeks blowfish-like and exhales. "It's not the yoga I'm concerned with."

Nothing in the medical literature suggests this is a viable course of action for fracture treatment, he tells me sternly. He enumerates in ghoulish detail the problems of letting someone poke bamboo needles in me when infection is the ever-present threat that could still have me wind up an amputee. I feel like a bad, bad little girl caught sticking bobby pins in electrical sockets. He is not wrong, nor is he small-minded. I have come to believe he is a good surgeon and a thorough doctor, who routinely takes a half hour or more discussing treatment with me. I never feel he shuts me out of the process, but I have in effect shut him out by not discussing this with him before I did it. Still, the issue we are dealing with is my body and how I will be able to function in the world. In the kingdom of Me, he is high council, but I have the crown.

While the soft tissue seems to be healing there is no new bone growth, and my current rod is nearly at the "failure rate," meaning that the rod could break under the pressure of walking. If that were to happen it would not only be excruciating, but require a messy surgery to remove it, likely setting progress on my fracture back another year. I'll need another surgery soon to replace the rod with a thicker one. He uses the term "dinky nail," which I find an unexpected and charming use of colloquialism; I think he might be loosening up. He hopes that surgery will actually stimulate the body to produce bone, but if there is no growth, I'll need a bone graft, where marrow is sucked from one hip and plastered over the break. "Infection on top of that could"—he hesitates, I think it's for effect—"be a serious problem."

I promise not to let the cute Korean acupuncturist who plays Sting CDs while he works stick those pins in me or burn any moss again. I am lying, because even Dr. Mesna cannot deny that the skin around the wound looks better, the color in the leg more flesh-like and healthy. I know there is some risk, but I am coming to understand that my life is a process of calculating odds; given the options before me I do what makes the best sense for my survival at the moment. The acupuncturist is certified, he is recommended by people I have come to trust as being right about other things that make me feel better, and millions of people in Asia exist with this form of medicine as their primary means of health care. The evidence points to this being a good decision—I am beginning to bend my toes and flex my ankle back and forth, from side to side, and I can even bend my knee enough to sit in a semi cross-legged position on the ground. I need my crutches less and less and can walk with just the moon boot, so much better is my balance. More than that, I have stopped taking Vicodin every six hours. Sometimes I don't take it for two days in a row. This progress could just be a result of doing yoga or the natural process of the body healing on its own, but I afraid to tamper with the recipe. Maybe the acupuncture and chiropractor and breathing through my left nostril and milk with turmeric create some magical combination, a form of alchemy. If I quit any one thing, maybe all this will go away, maybe I will shrivel up and crawl back in to bed and stay there, reduced, diminished.

What I cannot really explain to anyone is what actually spurs this thirst for things mystic. I previously would have thought myself too hip, too cool, too smart to do anything but mock it all. But the truth is, when I put my hands together at the center of my chest, when I allow myself to bow deeply, pressing my forehead to the floor, I invariably have this image of a huge glacier suddenly cracking, falling into a blue mirror of ocean and floating away. It's more than a mental rerun of something I saw on the Discovery channel. I actually feel a chipping away, a melting, piece by piece. I think of my mother on her knees, praying in Latin, the translation of the words long forgotten to her so that prayer is simply a current of sounds.

Even before Harley trampled me I believed myself to be broken, misshapen, and feared this was the way I would be for the rest of my existence. I have felt this way for as long as I can remember. I have worked out and dieted to become thinner, I have studied to become smarter, I have read Emily Post to pass, just to pass—it seems that I have predicated my entire life on the belief that I am a problem which must be fixed. And since the day Matt stepped into the rehab hospital, the paradigm of drug recovery has permeated our lives and underscored my sense of being malformed in some deep sense. "My disease," "your disease," our prison of illness... I keep hearing the words from the rehab sessions for family members, that I am "sicker than the addicts" in my life, that I have been co-starring in a warped play that will end as a tragedy for everyone concerned unless I too mend my ways.

Now I am having the experience of putting my hands together, breathing deep, and feeling that I am enough. My human self. I am all right. I have everything I need to live, broken leg and all. It's as if this is the knowledge my body has always had, but for the first time in my life I am hearing it, sensing it, comprehending it.

■ ■ ■

The word "mystic" comes from a verb that simply means to close one's eyes and lips. I have taken from that an idea of what it is to pray. The way I do this is to shut my eyes and pretend I am a kid again, sitting on the rocky bank of the Stillaguamish River in the summer, watching the water go by. Written on the surface are my thoughts, and I read them as they pass downriver. Edward's question is one that runs by on a more or less continual basis. *What we're really talking about is faith. Do you have it?*

A certain ironic stance is the religion of my generation. Belief and faith are just another way to say ignorant and deluded, or so I have always thought. I have never had a concept of what God meant, but now I have an inkling that God must be something like the feeling of gratitude, to wake up every day and be struck with the beauty of the strangest things, like the shape of a dog's paw, or the smell of orange juice.

■ ■ ■

I would like to say that my happily-ever-after comes now, that as a newly-minted bodhisattva I am wise and caring. But this is not what happens.

III.

A horse makes a woman difficult.

P art of my day now includes stopping at the barn. Juan puts Harley in the cross ties for me and then brings out a brush from my tack box. I stand near Harley, stroking his coat around his face and neck, not really grooming, that's an energetic process that requires some muscle, a sort of dance, being able to move in close and smoothly work a brush and curry. I avoid getting too near his legs, am still leery, aware that I can't move fast enough and don't have enough balance to be truly safe around a horse. Should he spook or kick at a fly I could be hurt. But as he brings his head down for the treats I always carry, I put my nose close enough to feel the thick hair that grows on the inside of his ears, soft like the edges of a powder puff. While I brush I talk into his ear, telling him everything I don't say to people.

I've heard it said that horses are substitutes for men. To me, horses are not men. They are beings whose emotional dependability can be charted. Harley, as was Goober before him, as was Gabe, as was Sunny, as was Breezy, as was Big Red, all the way back to my first pony, Mickey Merry Legs, is clear about what makes him happy and unhappy and he never, ever, wavers from that. That is not to say that horses are at all alike in their personalities. Harley, for instance, loves to be brushed and fussed over, will even fall asleep as the whiskers on his muzzle are trimmed with an electric clipper. Breezy would not tolerate anything beyond knocking the dust off his hide. Harley hates the sound of AM radio. Gabe liked mariachi bands, would collect himself beneath me and prance in what felt like a dance.

Admitting this to anyone would just give more ammunition to the argument that there is a sexual appeal between women and horses, that we equestrians get off by straddling a big brute between our thighs. I have ridden all my life and have yet to orgasm as a result—in fact sitting a horse correctly produces bruises and chafing, swelling and soreness. I am so tired of hearing about this bestiality from men and from other women who either aren't self-aware or are afraid to be honest. The appeal of horses is so much more threatening than that.

Little girls with their bouncing pigtails, grinning faces and Lilliputian bodies look so cute as they ride ponies, but a serious metamorphosis is actually occurring. These girls are beginning to understand that which men historically have always known. They are tasting what it means to move freely with great power, and they are developing an appetite for mobility. They are learning not to take no for an answer, even when that no comes from a being with one hundred times their strength. Riding is not the experience the girls will have when they get older and can drive a car, because their horses will nicker for them and will show affection and will favor them over others. A girl will work hard to earn her horse's loyalty, and this will be returned, and that is the dynamic she will come to expect of all others in her life. If a girl begins riding at an early age and continues until she is grown, all of this will be ingrained in her. In fact her bones themselves will be shaped by it.

There is no way around it: A horse makes a woman difficult. The French knew this and called equestriennes "amazones." Amazones were nothing less than a separate "race" of female. This race was composed of equal part female, male, and animal, a spellbinding "centauress," transforming the myth of Centaur, the Greek image of a people that stood for drunkenness and violence, its roots in stories about the brutal Kassite tribes of Iran in the second millennium B.C., who rode into the Near East bringing horses and decadence. The French saw the amazone as dangerous, a knife poised at the seam of the social fabric, because of her mobility. Mobility suggested sexual promiscuity, which in turn implied a certain brazen power, something to be feared.

This power is what we are ultimately falling in love with as little girls, as we beg our mommies for pony rides at the state fair, lie in bed looking at our Misty of Chincoteague posters, hugging our Breyer horse figurines, in our heads constructing arguments for why we will positively die if we don't get to have riding lessons.

Gurmukh has taken it on as a personal mission to see that I am healed, and to prove wrong all predictions on the ultimate functionality of my leg. "Western doctors are not bad, don't think I'm saying that. I mean, how great was it that they could put you back together?" she says, her hand over mine, then leans her turban in as if to share a secret. "It's just that sometimes they're... limited... in what they believe to be possible."

With little more than two months until the surgery to replace the "dinky nail" Gurmukh introduces me to John Hanrahan, an Olympic-wrestler-turned-personal-trainer who is intrigued by the challenge my injury presents. He develops special weight-training exercises to help strengthen my leg and restore some vigor to the rest of me. I like him immediately and our rapport is instant, him like the older brother I used to wish I had. At our first workout I am hesitant, imagine the rod in my leg cracking if I do much more than walk. But his competence transfers to me a certain amount of security, and we move slowly through some gentle movements using his hand or a wide elastic band for resistance. John starts calling a few times a week.

"Let's get you back in the gym, girl."

"John, I'm going to have to owe you."

"Pay me when we run the L.A. Marathon," he answers. "Just meet me after yoga, all right?"

Mike calls to give me an assignment. "How would you like to interview Bruce Lee before he became famous?" He is calling me because I used to have a thing for Chinese action movies, took boxing classes and was one of the few women he knew besides his girlfriend who would watch the Ultimate Fight Challenge on cable with him. I point out there are a couple problems with this assignment. One being Bruce Lee is already famous, and, two, quite dead.

"Gee, thanks for the update. Do you want to hear what I have to say or not?" There's a former Navy SEAL who has developed a revolutionary approach to the martial arts, he thinks the guy might make a good article.

Immediately I imagine a screaming boot camp drill sergeant in a judo gi. I could not be more disinterested if Mike were proposing that I write "Root Canals: Up Close and Personal." Still, I am working for my horse and to keep up my half of the bills, so I say yes.

It occurs to me when I meet him that lately I have been consistently wrong about almost all my preconceptions of people. The SEAL is not a walking cliché. He is soft spoken, well read, and his ideas do make an interesting topic for Mike's magazine. When he invites me to see one of his classes I accept, and that is how I find myself walking with him, about to across a street in Burbank to a park where several of his students wait, leaning on one crutch in a Tiny Tim way. I am talking, looking up at him, and suddenly I feel an excruciating jolt that seems as if my leg has been banged with a hammer; I didn't gauge how deep the curb went and I have tripped. I get a sickening sense of losing my balance, losing my crutch, and hurling face first toward the street.

He catches me before I hit, scooping me up and collecting me in his arms so that I am cradled against his chest. I allow myself a fraction of a moment to relax before he puts me down. There is a feeling of rescue, an intense relief. I savor it. Then I become profoundly self-conscious.

"Thanks. Did I mention that I'm a professional klutz?" I say in my aren't-I-charming-this-happens-all-the-time voice.

He gives me a tight, polite smile and we continue on

for several steps not saying anything. He turns to me when we reach the other side of the street.

"Listen," he says his tone serious. "I don't know you very well, and forgive me if this is none of my business, but I don't think you're a klutz. It seems to me that you don't care enough about yourself to pay attention to what you're doing. That's why you keep getting hurt."

I could not feel more nonplussed if he had just reached out and slapped me across the face. I have that I-left-my-diary-open feeling, kind of queasy yet mad at the same time. He's just gazing at me with a look that seems to mean, It's OK, I know I'm right. I have an urge to smack him. *If I wanted your opinion I'd beat it out of you*, a favorite saying in my family. My mother dated a string of these special-forces types before she met my stepfather, and they all had the same air of being convinced of their absolute authority regarding literally everything on the planet.

"I'm sorry if I spoke out of turn," he finally says. "It's just that I am trained to be observant."

"Swell. They gave you Superman x-ray vision in SEAL team?" I snap at him as I continue forward with my head down, eyes focused on the ground.

"No. We just leap tall buildings," he says.

"The few, the proud, the opinionated."

"No. It's 'Admit nothing, deny everything, and make counter-accusations.'"

"Whatever." But I can't help but laugh.

■ ■ ■

I observe his class for a short time then excuse myself, saying I have another appointment. On the drive home through Malibu Canyon, I pull the truck over and sit in the cab with the radio turned off. I watch for a long time the circle of two ravens as they spiral from the height of the canyon's jagged walls down to the crooked muddy line of creek below.

His comment still resonates. Where is it written on me

that I have been careless with my life? Is it in the tilt of my head, the way I talk with my hands, the slump of my shoulders? I suppose I thought that by doing yoga postures, eating lentil stew and taking cold showers for two months that I had already remedied a life history. This is addict logic, one fix and I'll be fine, when really it takes the rest of a life of constant tending to undo what has already been set in motion. There is a reason they use the terms "yoga practice," "spiritual practice."

All at once I feel overwhelmed by the task ahead of me, to sift through which feelings are mine, which really belong to my mother and grandmother. I put my head on the steering wheel and shut my eyes.

■ ■ ■

Gram was the kind of woman who was so beautiful when she was young that she hated the look of her own skin as she aged. Her eyes were a shade of dark brown that appeared black. *Black Irish*. She could count to a hundred in French and insult you, *Taisez-vous imbécile*. She wanted to go to business school after high school; when she came home and told her father this, he was angry and shocked, and he hit her. Women didn't do things like that. She didn't leave the house for a whole weekend. Sometimes when she told this she reported that her father only cried at hearing her desire to attend business school. Perhaps he did both.

Whatever the truth was, it is certain that she eloped with my grandfather soon after that incident, a young man whom she had known for three months. He was a flute player and a bus driver and for a while they owned a diner where she overcooked the meat. They divorced in the '50s; he ran off with a plain-looking woman who already had two daughters. *Peggy had the biggest ass*. It was a detail she could never reconcile with the rules she thought she knew about what men find valuable in women. He left my grandmother with their one child, my mother, to raise. For the rest of her life her voice would shake when she said his name. She'd tell my mother, *Your dirty rotten son of a bitch father. You look just like him.*

Being a divorcée did get Gram into business, at least; she became a lingerie buyer for a department store and traveled to New York City regularly. *All by myself on the train.* She once stayed at the Waldorf Astoria and shared an elevator with Ronald Reagan when he was still just that actor in *Bedtime for Bonzo.* He noticed what a great looking-dame she was, she said. First: He smiled at her. Then: He asked her for a drink. And: She said no, she wasn't that kind of lady, the kind that would have a drink with a handsome, famous man she'd just met. Of course she was that kind of lady, so I have no idea what really happened. Maybe he did not notice what a great looking dame she was. *You lying two-bit shyster,* she'd yell at the television when he was president. She would tune into State of the Union addresses just for the pleasure of getting mad. *How you got elected I'll never know.*

My mother spent her childhood trying to figure out what she had personally done to make her father leave and make her mother so unhappy. Her hair was the color of new pennies and curled in ringlets around her face. She memorized poetry from Kipling to recite to the adults who didn't have time to hear it, she took ballet and rode an old horse named Salty. By the time she got to high school she declared herself a rebel and dyed her hair black. In the pictures of her yearbook she looks like the prototype for Stockard Channing's take on the Rizzo character in *Grease.* She too got sent on a Greyhound to spend the summer with Aunt Gay and Uncle Roy in Washington. After high school she joined the Air Force and distinguished herself by having the highest IQ score of any enlistee that year. She requested assignment to New Mexico because she'd read about it in Zane Grey novels. She felt comfortable in the openness of the high desert, liked the fact that you can see things coming.

After four years as a WAF, Mom returned home to work as a cocktail waitress and a nurse's aide so she could save money. That and the GI Bill would get her to college for sure. It was the '60s, things were possible. She wanted to be a doctor. An internist, or possibly ER, she couldn't decide. She was in her first semester of college when she went to a party and spied a tall, fair Italian man dancing with a blonde.

I knew some Italian thanks to the crowd I ran around with in high school.

What did you say?

I said "ciao" and he asked me if I spoke Italian. I told him, "Soltanto nel mio quare," which I think means "Only in my heart." Might have been a Mario Lanza lyric, I forget.

Very cool.

I'm a classy broad, what can I tell you.

She had a black, three-quarter length dress, with spaghetti straps that had the habit of falling off her shoulders. Mom also has this way of arching her right eyebrow. The blonde had no chance.

The Italian left after a few months. Then I arrived. She had to rethink her medical career. Nurse was the next best, most possible option, but even to do that she had to move in with her mother. My mother ranks three events in her life by their order of severity, during each of which she thought her life was ending: Her parents' divorce; the death of her husband, my step-father; and the day she found out she was pregnant with me. I could have been named Calamity.

■ ■ ■

I think about why it felt so good to be caught when I tripped. To not have to pick myself up again.

■ ■ ■

Two days later I am driving down the Pacific Coast Highway to an evening yoga class when the whirl of red lights begins to flash behind me. Traffic cops on the Pacific Coast Highway are a constant plague, locusts in the wheat field. They're bad enough if you drive a Jaguar or a BMW, but if you happen to be in a dented Toyota truck with a tailgate covered in bumper stickers for punk bands with names like "Johnny Cats" and

"Man Will Surrender," you should expect to be swarmed. I pull to the berm and brace myself for the interrogation. License, insurance please, where are you headed, please step out of the car. They are always looking to catch someone with drugs; the truck fits a profile. I breathe deep and reassure myself those days are gone, there's nothing to fear. Still, I check the ashtray. It's empty.

I roll down the window as I hear the crunching sound of feet along gravel. The officer shines a flashlight in my face, he just a dark silhouette in back of the light. "Here you are, sir," I say as I hand over my license and insurance card. It is useless to ask the charge, they have a hundred ways you can be guilty and not know it.

A hand takes the items. "Are you aware that your registration tag is not current?"

"No sir," I say. "This is my husband's truck. I am just driving it because I can't use my own car." I tell him I have a busted leg in a brace, pointing down to it. "See?"

The officer lowers the flashlight and peers in the side window. He is about my age, blond moustache, side part. His eyes scan the littered interior, the dust on the dashboard, the single crutch next to me. He asks if I have the registration paper, so I search through the overstuffed glove compartment, pushing past cassette tapes, receipts for oil changes, ancient check stubs, until I find an expired registration with Matt's name on it.

The officer regards it for a moment, then passes it back to me. "I'm not going to cite you ma'am," he says, and a wave of relief crashes over me. "But," he adds, "can I be blunt?"

I have never heard a police officer ask permission to be blunt, so I can't image what's coming. "Please," I tell him.

"Ma'am, if you were my wife with a broken leg, I sure wouldn't let you drive around in a car like this," he says. "Tell your husband he needs to take better care of you."

What do you say after a comment like this? Thank you? I nod and roll up the window, wait for him to get back in the patrol car so I can pull back out to the highway. How dare he. Cro-Magnon. Like I am the little woman and need my big, strong husband to protect me from the nasty, scary world. Like I'm incapable of doing it myself. What an idiot. He doesn't know us. He doesn't have one idea how we are with each other.

Only after I mentally call the cop every filthy insult I know—an extensive list, it takes a while—do I start to cry. I see Matt's Raphaelite face, the smoothness of his skin, think how long it's been since I have seen him look happy. Dragging himself out of bed before dawn so he can make the forty-five-mile drive to work. No friends from before, and the people from rehab back in the orbit of their own worlds. Our life only a gray space between what used to be and what might come next. He is trying to make sense of his life. He is doing the very best that he knows. And although I want it to be, I want more than anything for it to be, what I cannot say to myself is: It is not enough for me. But I can't demand more. It's just not fair. And I don't know how.

I have had this feeling since I was a little girl: I am standing on a plank, my heels off the edge. Behind me is a cavernous drop, at the bottom sharp needles and broken bottles. A net? There is no net. I have to keep moving forward.

■ ■ ■

When I arrive home I check my computer, find an email from the Navy SEAL. He says he noticed I have developed a walk where I turn my bad leg slightly out at an angle and push off in a rolling motion.

> You'll get hip problems that way, I would like to suggest some techniques for walking normally. I would be happy to have you come back to class.

I think he's joking. I tell him that's a good one, but that I feel lucky to walk as well as I do. No solid bone, tendons, nerves, muscles cut. I walk fine, considering.

He replies to my email instantly:

> Considering what? Considering yourself handicapped? Your definitions of yourself and your limits on what you consider possible are the only handicaps you have.

I stare at the screen, debate whether I should just delete the message. Wonder why today is the day strange men want to offer their opinions.

To be caught. A net.

I start to add up all the people who have extended help to me in some form or other since that day in the canyon; I tick three dozen names off the top of my head. Perhaps I have confused a cocoon with a net. No one is guaranteed to be insulated from the work of surviving, but those hands extended form their own net; it's always up to you to do the weaving.

I write:

> Thanks for your offer to help. Can I come to your class next week and get some pointers?

It is the last week of May. A grey marine layer blankets the coast but the San Fernando Valley roasts under a clear sky. I am being wheeled into the operating room of Kaiser Hospital for the surgery where Dr. Mesna will replace the "dinky nail" with what I have termed the "macho nail." The macho nail is light green, not as attractive as the robin's egg blue of the current one, I note this to an orthopedic technician I know from my many weekly visits. "You can't have everything," he says. He takes my hand as we wheel into the room. I have asked him to, since the nurses made me leave my sandalwood mandala in the pre-op center. Fingering the round wooden beads had been its own Valium.

"Nervous?" he asks.

"Nope. Just wanted to hold hands."

"Oh, I forget. You're a pro at this by now." He smiles. He's losing his hair, it gives his smile more face to cover.

In the operating room they're blasting "Sweet Home Alabama" through a boom box, it's a party, come on in. I realize how comfortable I feel in the hospital, I know the lingo, joke with the staff. I have a flash of anxiety that has nothing to do with the fact that I am about to undergo a surgery during which my knee joint could crack from the trauma of the rod insertion, or hairline fractures could develop in the tibia from the violence of the placement. More disturbing at this moment is the realization that, some day, I will not need any more surgeries, and so will lose the part I play in this ongoing theater. I will have to leave my role as the injured person and again assume the identity of someone who can literally carry her own weight.

The music changes to Natalie Merchant and I know Dr. Mesna is in the room; he has a thing for female singer-songwriters. Carly Simon is a favorite. "Ms. Dunn," he says brightly, just his blue-masked face over me, those cereal box eyes. He brings up to my view the electric screwdriver he'll use to remove the bolts at my ankle holding the rod in place. He revs it a few times. Vroom, vroom. "Ready to get started?"

"Is that a Black and Decker? Can you build me some bookshelves when you finish?"

His mask moves. I think he smiles. "Did I mention I worked as a carpenter during college?"

"Construction workers make the best orthopedists," I tell him. The anesthesiologist has arrived and she is telling me something about my IV. The lights suddenly appear more brilliant, Dr. Mesna's voice like he is talking to me down a long tiled hall. He is giving a lecture about angles, carpentry.

■ ■ ■

In post-op I come out of anesthesia slowly, aching. Feel as if I have been drugged and dragged behind a car. I get shivery, my teeth clack. Dr. Mesna is beside me. "Everything went smoothly," he says. "No complications..." he continues to talk. Three days of recovery in the hospital. Back up on crutches by tomorrow.

Shut up David, I want to say. Instead, "Can I have some drugs?"

■ ■ ■

The pain is worse this time than any I can remember, a stabbing, twisting sensation with a tenacious grip. I wake up in the hospital room, bob in and out of sleep, somnolence like the tide. I keep fighting to break the surface. Gurmukh calls, says she prayed for me today. My mom calls, says I love you baby-doll. Each time my eyes open there seem to be new visitors in the chairs beside the bed. I collect a series of still shots: Renee in her black long sleeves. My friend Lola comes from her job at the library, talks about the basketball game showing on the room's television with the Navy SEAL who is stopping by. He brings carnations. Bernie in his blue smock enters the room. Hey Sunshine. Carryl says hi. John Hanrahan and Mike sit next to each other with backs straight, hands on the arm rests. More flowers. How are you feeling? Not up for a workout, John. Ha ha. Next week? OK.

I always hope Matt will fill the frame, but Lola reminds me he is at work. Yes, I knew that. He has to meet a friend from rehab. I knew that. He has a commitment to his sobriety group he cannot break. I knew that. Finally: "Sam, wake up, look, Matty's here," says Lola, her voice loud and cheerful, a pep squad of one. Thank God. His smooth skin, the brush of his goatee. I want to wake up but I am so tired, so achy. It is night, the lights of the room now yellowed and dim. He says, "Hey, I bought you a portable cd player." He puts the earphones to my head, the music faint.

Later, I feel a touch against my hair. I half open my eyes. He is leaning over me, trying to gently stroke the hair from my face with a small brush. His large hands tentative. There is something beautiful, mournful in his action. I shut my eyes and hope he continues. *Why didn't you come earlier?* I realize this is a touch I will recall for the rest of my life.

I cannot make sense of what comes next other than to say I start to experience that airless feeling from long ago with Gene and the Mercury Comet, the drawstring being pulled tight. *Mira, I still love you. Que paso?*

■ ■ ■

A few weeks after my last surgery I am driving in Culver City, and I pull up to an intersection to make a left hand turn. For a moment—or perhaps it is longer than a moment, perhaps minutes go by—I lose track of where I am. There are many factors involved: Vicodin taken several hours before for that stabbing pain, a cell phone, images from the archive of my life, like flipping pages in a photo album. Here is the first fish I caught. There is Matt in mirrored sunglasses. Tina and her spiky hairdo, reading a book in our college dorm. The white stripe in the dark tail of a buckskin gelding named Sunny. My mother pouring coffee, black, no cream. *Breakfast of Champions.*

Anyway, I hit a car in front of me.

It's not awful, a fender bender they call it. The first auto accident I have ever been involved in. Going only 10 miles an hour, luckily. The other driver surprised but not hurt. She had been stopped at the intersection in the turn lane. Didn't I see the light was red? No. Yes. I... I... have no way to justify myself.

But, wait, I tell myself. Hey, things happen. The environment we exist in is extremely forgiving, otherwise every stop light missed or speed limit exceeded would result in something bad happening. But that is not the case. I have a flash that maybe I have been dressing up with complicated rationales what is just the order of chance. You win some, you lose some. But even as I say this to myself I see the reams of abstracts I once pored over. People who attribute important events in life to chance, rather than making the association that something within their behavior had an influence, are more often involved in accidents. I remember the vow I make every day: *Sat Nam*, Truth is my Identity.

Only after we trade information and I get back in my car do my hands start to shake so badly I consider for a moment this is some kind of seizure. Petit mal would be the term, but no, it is merely an excess of adrenaline. This is the cue that I am terrified. Always before my accidents have involved only me, I have been the one to get hurt. This is the first time my actions have jeopardized the life of another person. I think, what if that has been a kid on a bike? A woman like me, unable to move fast while crossing the street?

More than that, I am angry with myself and ashamed, because I know too much now. I have the experience and the reasoning capabilities to know that if you take a Vicodin, talk on the cell phone and daydream, you're not just inviting risk. You're marrying it. I am recalling the study that found drivers with marital problems were more likely to have accidents around the time they filed for divorce. A somnambulist once, yes, but now this unconsciousness is a willful act.

I cannot get around this: I have to say out loud the words that have been running silently through my mind, because if I don't, I am not only a danger to myself. Maybe, next time, I will kill someone else.

■ ■ ■

Almost every woman I know has been in therapy at some time or other. When I ask for recommendations I receive so many phone numbers for psychiatrists, psychologists and family counselors I finally just say eeny-meeny-miney-moe.

I look at the number then change my mind, search through the papers where I have the numbers written and call the one for the therapist with experience in "family dynamics and addiction issues."

The therapist is a little man. His office a sleek design with modern furniture and a black couch. "Nice leather," I tell him. A rendering of Buddha hangs on the wall. The therapist sits leaning forward with his hands on his knees, wrinkles like tributary streams surround his brown eyes.

"Welcome," he says.

"I don't want to take up too much of your time," I begin. "I only have a couple of questions."

And then I burst into tears. I empty a Kleenex box. He hands me another.

Each July I to go to New York for business. Bruises from the surgery have turned to yellow and the fresh incision at my knee looks a healthy pink. I decide I'll go this year.

The flight from LAX to JFK is crowded as usual. Sitting to my right in coach class is Darla. It is only 30 minutes into the flight but already I know that, through some order of the universe, it is not by accident Darla is seated next to me. I look at her face and it is like seeing my own reflected in a series of funhouse mirrors, the warped suggestions of what could have been, maybe, but is not.

She is about 15 years older than I, a tall redhead in a broomstick skirt who has to have her right leg propped up on long flights. I say, that's funny, I have to have my left leg propped up. Why do you? And she says, Take a look at this, lifting her skirt high enough for me to see the gnarled bump on her leg at precisely the same point on the shin as the scar on my left leg. Bone infection, she says. Spiral fracture of the tibia, four years ago in a freak accident. I stepped onto a deck and a board broke and then my leg was caught and then, snap! The thing has still not healed.

"The other doctors want to amputate," she says.

"They always do," I concur.

Darla tells me she is on her way to New York to see a doctor who might be able to help. Well, that's not really why she's going. She's going because she just found her daughter who had been kidnapped by her ex-husband. Well, not really kidnapped, just taken away when she had this car accident and the kid was in the car and, bastard, how was that her fault?

It's a six-hour flight; I hear it all. Darla is a former stripper whose father was a cop who actually worked for the Mob. She tells me she knows she is an alcoholic and a drug addict but she is also a Jehovah's Witness who believes in karma and by the way does shiatsu massage on the side.

She says she graduated from medical school, or would have if there hadn't been that other time where she broke her wrist. There have been other car crashes, once the Jaws of Life, sprains, the concussions. Bruises? Girl, too many to count. Husbands troubles, honey? I've got two exes, you haven't seen anything yet. Scars on her wrists from suicide attempt number two, the one before with sixty-eight Excedrin PMs and a fifth of Wild Turkey. But nothing will kill her yet. Has killed her yet, excuse me. She has the worst luck. "People always say I'm such a klutz," she says, lines around her mouth from the smile that is always on her face.

She gives me a bookmark and a Watchtower pamphlet. "No, no," she protests gently when I say the carved wood of the bookmark is too nice to give to a stranger. "I want you to have it."

We both wear sterling silver rings, hers on her right-hand ring finger, mine on the left. "Here," I say, pulling mine off and extending it to her. "Let's trade." She takes hers from her finger and presses it into my palm. "I am glad you'll have this," she says. "That way you'll never forget the nice talk we had."

"Darla, I never will." I place a hand over hers.

■ ■ ■

New York is a gauntlet, a nightmare of stairs and uneven sidewalks. I press myself crab-like along walls as crowds pass by, I know what it feels like to be trampled and these crowds have that energy. Mentally I bless the sprawl of L.A., the wide freeways, mini-malls with parking in front.

My leg aches by the time I arrive at a meeting, my brow

wet with sweat. An editor friend winces when he sees me wobble slightly as I rise from a chair.

"It's hard for me to see you get around this way." He takes my arm, steadies me.

"I left my good legs at home," I joke but he does not smile back. He looks worried, and this jolts a little. At home everyone tells me how much improved I am, how well I am doing, and I realize they are measuring against the stages of my healing during the past ten months. But this man only has the mental picture of me before to contrast with the woman he sees in front of him now.

I have a panicked feeling, like I should think up something quick to prove I'm the same as always. *Original Formula! New Packaging!* But then I remember my carved wood bookmark and Darla, our lady of the perpetual trauma. Her red hair, our silver rings. What image of herself does she have in her head? What put that image there, and has it always been the same?

I think of the therapist sitting with his hands at his knees, my litany of questions.

What kind of a wife am I? What kind of a professional? What kind of a person am I? Well, what kind?

Perhaps you can try existing without a label for now. Try not knowing.

I hits me what he was talking about. If I give up the ideas of how I should be, then maybe, just maybe, I can make room for who I am.

"Here," I say to my friend, "please take my hand. All this walking is wearing me out."

■ ■ ■

When the end of Matt and me comes there is little yelling, just the thud of finality, an aching strain of regret. *Not with a bang but a whimper.* It is the evening I return from New York.

"I was the sick one." He says this sitting on the couch, his lands in his lap. He is looking at me with those huge hazel eyes; how beautiful they are. "Now you're the sick one, and I just want you to get well. For yourself. Not for me. It's too late for that."

I am not sick, I think. Angry, but not sick. In pain, but not sick. Confused, but not sick. Still I cannot say these things to him, words choke in my throat, like chewing ice. They said I would not be able to run again, but this is exactly what I do. I run out on him rather than force the words from my mouth and stick around to see what happens. *If it seems like I'm free it's because I'm always running.* Jimi Hendrix said that.

Matt packs my Nissan sedan; it hurts but I can push in the clutch now. He fills the car to the roof with luggage, a few books, my laptop computer. There is room for just one dog, my pug Ming. The big dog, Nika, stays with her dad. It is a modern arrangement. He fills the ashtray with $150 in cash. Walking-around money, he says. No, he doesn't say that. I think that. Gram used to give me walking-around money, a quarter when I went out so I would always be able to call home.

I drive to Renée's house for the night. She doesn't ask questions. Her cats regard me coolly with their green eyes, as if they have seen it all already. I sleep for twelve hours in Renee's guest bed, Ming curled into my side, ensconced in the frothy comforter. In the morning, late, after coffee, I move to Mary Ellen's house at the top of a crest in the Santa Monica Mountains. Both her sons are gone, she has an extra bedroom. She's waiting at the door, puts an arm around my shoulders. Why did he stay? Why were you the one to leave? She wants to know. I always leave, I tell her. It always feels safer to keep moving.

"This is home for as long as it takes you to it figure out," she says, then proceeds to the kitchen. "Eating will make you feel better."

I think nothing will make me feel better.

■ ■ ■

The room Mary Ellen has given me has a twin bed with a pine frame, and a window that looks out onto the roan-colored hills of Calabasas, all covered in a nubby spread of shrunken oaks and the occasional thrust of yucca. I spent days just lying in that twin bed, like in those first weeks after the accident. This is the real break; my leg was just practice in seeing what I thought was inseparable from me become a distinct and unattached entity.

Lying across the white bedspread with my check against the thick cotton pillow case, I think often about what Lucia said. *God touches us with a feather, then if we don't listen he starts throwing bricks.* Ironic those words should come from her, the most renowned professional female boxer on the planet, who puts herself on the line physically every day of her life. *Aren't you scared sometimes?* I asked her once. *No, not any more. I learned to listen.* As a teenage champion in Holland, she was almost killed in a kickboxing match when she was pitted against a man. Her managers and trainers wanted her to, it would make a great show, they said. She listened to everyone but herself, and the man knocked her cold. More than ten years later, she has not been knocked out again. Nor has she lost a single match.

I think of Harley standing over me, the rush of my blood, its fresh color, the impossible white of my bones exposed to air. This was the brick. Finally, this was the brick.

■ ■ ■

Edward finds me at Mary Ellen's after not talking for more than a month. I did not leave a forwarding number. I am worried he will be disappointed with me, my pending divorce, he's been married more than twenty years and believes in the institution. He says no, there is never any room for judgment. "What this means is that a space has opened in your life," he says. "Resist the urge to fill it right back up again. See what comes in naturally."

That evening I go to yoga. At the end of class we sit with our hands at the center of our chests, eyes shut. Slowly the voices around me build, singing the song that always comes at the end. The words form an odd lullaby. *May the longtime sun shine upon you, all love surround you, and the pure light within you guide your way on.* I hear it now as an incantation of release, a way to honor the act of letting go. At the finish I bow my head to the floor and leave it there a long time, listening to the others as their bare feet pad across the wood to the door, until I am the last one in the room. My tears form a dead sea. I taste the brine of them with my tongue.

It is a slow process, assembling a life. I search for pieces that fit, like putting together a puzzle. I begin again with the things I know: I wake up. I feed my dog. I work on magazine assignments from the little room at Mary Ellen's. "Keep breathing," Gurmukh says on the phone. "If you only do one thing, keep breathing."

■ ■ ■

It is perhaps a week after I move into Mary Ellen's. I am at the barn, grooming Harley. I lay my hand across his smooth back, rub the ridge of wither. He has an old scar at the top where the hair has grown in white. Much like the white lines of my own scars. Suddenly I have the intense urge to know again the view from up there; the world has always made sense to me from the vantage point of a horse's back. Perhaps, if I sit there for just for a moment, I will see everything clearly.

On the spot I hatch a plan to tack Harley up and just sit on him while he stands. To do this I need to enlist Juan's help. Because I walk with a rolling motion, left foot slightly turned out because I don't have the power to push off in a normal stride, I can't manage the steep steps up to the tack room. Even without the added weight of my saddle and bridle I risk either losing my balance or stepping down hard on my bad leg. The pain of that would suck the breath out of me and cause spots to appear in front of my eyes. I know this because about a month ago I wanted to go inside to grab a curry comb, and couldn't make it past the first step.

Juan is at first wary but finally agrees when I promise not to do more than sit for five minutes on Harley's back. "Cross my heart," I tell him, making the motion. "No problemo."

After Juan saddles Harley he leads him to the mounting block. I put my riding helmet on; it seems to me like putting on a seat belt to sit in a parked car, but, still, I am not so arrogant to ignore that caution is a worthwhile investment. Then the problem is how to actually get high enough so that I can slide on to his back: Juan holds Harley's bridle with one hand and steadies me with the other as I crawl onto the mounting block on hands and knees. Reaching the saddle I steady myself there, then lean my weight over Harley, finally swinging my moon boot across his back and righting myself in the saddle.

Surprisingly, there is no fear, only the rush of feeling able-bodied again. It is as if I am seven years old once more and have been set astride Big Red, intoxicated for the first time with a sense of the possible.

Harley stands quietly, flicks his ears as if waiting for directions. *What now, boss?* My leg immediately starts to throb from the pressure of hanging but I ignore it for now. My hands run over his shoulders, I inhale the smell of him, the scent of oil and dried sweat, a single green stalk of alfalfa tangled in his mane. I grab a handful, the wiry black strands. How like suture thread; I never noticed that before.

I am happy, truly happy. Then Drew spots me.

"Sam!" his voice is strained, the tone chastising, "I can't be responsible for this." He walks quickly from the other side of the barn, talking the whole time about insurance liability, what if, what if. He looks pale, in disbelief, as if I am straddling a dragon and not a horse.

"Drew," I answer caustically, "I take responsibility for my own actions. I am not going to sue you. Get over it."

But it is too late. The magic fairy dust has evaporated and I see what he sees: A woman who was nearly killed and who still is not healed, up again on the animal that injured her. I become aware just how ridiculous I look, my floppy sweatshirt, leg brace, helmet matting down my hair, and of the tremendous size of my thoroughbred, the distance from his back down to the hard topsoil. *Humpty Dumpty sat on a wall.* I am seized by an image of myself as an eggshell.

I apologize to Drew. "You meant well, I know," I tell him. "I didn't mean to alarm you." Getting down scares me, even with Juan's help. Harley makes a small step to the side and I clutch his neck, easing myself down with my left leg bent, reaching toward the ground with my right foot, landing all my weight there.

On the twenty-minute drive back to Mary Ellen's house I think about my mom, how that fall from Becky frightened her so deeply she would never again venture onto the back of a horse. I never understood it before, but now I realize how that becomes possible. I feel a sense of sinking, being drawn down into a dark place, a current of mourning.

Then, like breaking the surface, I feel a rush of air in my lungs. No, I say out loud to myself. No no no no. I will not lose this. I will not.

■ ■ ■

My mother sends care packages: Canned green chiles, a refrigerator magnet etched with the saying, "Hang in there, Pussycat," lacy, peach-colored bras and underwear ordered from the Hanes discount catalog, "Kathy" and "Peanuts" comics she has cut out of the daily newspaper, a horoscope where it is confirmed that people born under the sign of Leo are, in fact, having a bad month. Everyone else, including the therapist I start to see once a week, gives me the same advice. "Exist in a state of not knowing." "Don't make any decisions." "Examine your feelings, see where they originate." This is all murderously difficult to do. At one point I stand alone on Mary Ellen's balcony, crying, staring down the rough hillside. I think would rather fall down this incline than feel what I am feeling right now. Then it occurs to me: This is exactly what I have been doing my entire life.

■ ■ ■

A friend introduces me to an essayist named Mike Heher. He turns out to be Father Mike Heher, Catholic priest. Funny how things come around. Back with the Catholics where I started, or, more rightly said, didn't start. We begin a correspondence about writing, religion, updates on what celebrities I have interviewed and were they nice.

I ask him in one communication, What do I do with my life from this point forward? Just tell me and I'll do it. I feel like he has already taken this test and knows the answers for the final. He writes:

> Someone once said that life must be lived forward but can only be understood looking backward. I think we have to endure much before we can see how God has guided our steps. To do it prematurely is to make as real only what you wish were real. I am of the providence-is-a-mystery school. By that I mean that human and divine life is so complex and inter-related that it is almost impossible to see how God acts or why. I don't see how the suffering of innocents or the dreadful acts of the holocaust have any place in God's providence. But I believe that God is there, even there. I live providence as a belief and a question. Perhaps this will get you started.

D r. Mesna is not surprised when I tell him of my recent split from my husband. Slow-healing fractures have the effect of a tornado in a person's life, he tells me. Often jobs are lost, patients go bankrupt, and marriages fail.

"Thanks for the heads up on that one."

"You're one of the lucky ones," he replies, instantly turning my self-pity around in the rational, let-me-explain-the-facts-to-you manner I have come to rely on. He says serious fractures like mine more often befall men who ride motorcycles or work in manual labor, meaning they lose their earning power, sometimes permanently. At least I am a writer who can work from bed. Think of that French writer, the one who ate the cookies.

"Proust," I say, glad for once to be on a subject with him where I am the resident authority.

My appointments are down to once every six weeks. The soft tissue healing is superior, I have more flexibility and less swelling than he anticipated, but my x-rays show the bone is still not producing any significant signs of "union." We are nearing the one-year anniversary of my accident, and it looks as if the surgery replacing the rod didn't stimulate growth as hoped. He schedules a bone graft surgery for the month after next, a prospect I dread because even Dr. Mesna says the section of hip from which the marrow is drawn will be terribly sore and ache. Now I will have to heal from that, too. I think about being back in bed, giving up the mobility I have finally achieved, not being able to move around my horse, do any yoga or work out with

John. I feel like a failure, that the effort I have put toward my healing hasn't been good enough. The furtive drinking of Diet Coke, the mornings I have fallen asleep during my meditation. My effort at healing not unlike the effort I put toward marriage. Less than perfect. Next week in my ninety-minute session the therapist will ask why I question myself and not the alternative therapies, or my husband's role in our marital collapse. Maybe by next week I'll think of a good answer.

Upset and defeat must register on my face. "I remember my first divorce," Carryl says right away when Dr. Mesna leaves to see another patient. "You'll be fine." She shuts the examining room door for a woman-to-woman, as is our habit now when I come for my check-ups. "Here," she says, pulling something from the pocket of her smock. "I just went back for my son's wedding. You remember the one? Take a look at these pictures of my grandkids…"

■ ■ ■

After yoga class a few days later, Gurmukh pulls me aside to talk. "I've been thinking so much about your leg," she says. I had called her after the appointment with Dr. Mesna to report the bad news of the bone graft surgery. "Will you be my tiny pet?"

"Excuse me?"

She laughs and explains that "tiny pet" only means that I will be the subject she works with when she attends a day-long teacher training workshop led by GuruDev Singh, renowned in the Sikh community internationally as a master of Sat Nam Rasayan. Sat Nam Rasayan is a healing meditation practiced among the Sikhs, which, very roughly explained, is where a practitioner meditates on your problem with you. GuruDev is Mexican by birth, and once joked that his students should use their loved ones like "tiny pets" to experiment on. The word he had been looking for was "mice," but the phrase stuck.

This meditation is not the laying-on of hands or faith healing; in fact the practitioner doesn't even touch you, doesn't even have to see you. I think the idea is more akin to the common practice of saying a prayer for someone in the hope that prayer resonates in the cosmos and produces a result. Sat Nam Rasayan is supposed to work for broken hearts, bad backs, cancer, troubled minds, any and all manner of ills.

I had experimented with this months ago with a friend of Gurmukh's, Hargo Pal Kaur Khalsa, whom the American Sikhs recognize as one of the country's few expert practitioners of this esoteric study. I remember Hargo Pal told me to "release an intention into the universe." I lay flat out on my back in corpse pose—the easiest yoga posture to master, I keep my palms up—and sunk into an relaxed twilight that was not quite sleep and not quite meditation. I tried to think of some really great intention—world peace, an end to nuclear proliferation, another Bruce Springsteen/E Street Band reunion tour—something many people, not just myself, would benefit from. But, for some reason, what repeated through my mind was the image of Michelangelo's painting in the Sistine Chapel, where the knotty finger of Adam and the hand of God touch tip to tip, the spark of creation where they meet.

I felt deeply relaxed when we were finished, but the sensation was no different than waking from a good night's sleep. I made a note to save money and just sleep. Still, who am I to say there's nothing to it? There are more things between heaven and earth, indeed. "Of course," I tell her. "Always happy to be a tiny pet."

■ ■ ■

Fifty people dressed all in white are sitting with legs folded in lotus position or are lying prone, quiet as stones. Blankets, mats and downy sheepskins form a dreamy patchwork over the floor in a space the size of a high school classroom. GuruDev, a large man with a long black beard and glasses, sits on a mound of cushions surrounded by flowers and a bowl of fruit, at which he seems to occasionally nibble. I am snuggled among sheepskin and a thick cotton blanket. I doze lightly, but each time I shut my eyes I have the Michelangelo image again. I try to think why this is. I have never been to Italy, but perhaps it is some genetic memory passed from my unknown Italian father, my only inheritance. GuruDev lives in Rome and has flown in to give this workshop, so perhaps my brain is making an association. That, however, doesn't account for the first time I experienced this mental picture those months ago, long before I knew anything about this teacher.

I figure that the meditation is some powerful form of placebo effect, because for the last few hours I really have had less pain. In fact, no pain. One theory for why a placebo could work is that it lowers a person's anxiety level, and therefore reduces the expectation of pain. The thinking in Western medicine is that a placebo effect becomes profound when a person's belief in the treatment is combined with the confidence and enthusiasm displayed by those administering the treatment. On the other hand, perhaps GuruDev is actually subtly rearranging divine energy in the cosmos to lessen my suffering. Who knows. Does it matter? He seems like a nice man, with large, soulful brown eyes and the tendency to give a belly-shaking laugh. I am sure if he could personally lessen the suffering of each of us, he would. Perhaps that intention is enough.

At a break Gurmukh takes me up to the cushioned platform to introduce me to GuruDev. I have prepared the usual story about my leg injury, expecting he will ask. He doesn't.

"Your shoulder," he points to my left side. "What is the problem?" This catches me off guard and I stammer for a moment, collecting my thoughts. Yes, this is the shoulder that was dislocated and popped back in. It gives me the occasional twinge and ache and is weaker than the other shoulder, but I had almost forgotten about it, so much has healing my leg been the focus of attention.

"Tell me about your horse. I rode the horses when I was a boy. In Mexico. Oh, I loved it," he says, his accent decorated by his native Spanish, further complicated by years of speaking

Italian. I tell him how Harley had been a racehorse bound for slaughter when he was rescued by a woman, who then gave him to me. I try to make myself sound like a rescuer too, telling him about the money and time I put into the broken-down racehorse.

GuruDev stops me, waves a finger in my direction like correcting a naughty child. "No," he says, his voice so soft I have to lean in to hear him. "You did not save him. He saved you. He is your *guru*. You know what means *guru*? *Guru* means that which brings you from darkness into the light."

■ ■ ■

When the workshop ends I drive straight to the stable. By the time I reach Harley's paddock, the honeyed light of dusk is already blending into one of those blue Pacific nights. I watch him silently while he chomps at his hay, a hind foot cocked lazily to the side. "OK guru," I tell him finally, leaning on the cold metal of the pipe coral gate. "Just don't get any ideas about me putting fresh flowers and incense in your manger."

As if in reply Harley he looks over to me, sticks his tongue out and flaps it against his muzzle before swinging his head over the gate. Then with that rubber nose he rifles through my jacket pockets to take his usual booty of peppermint candies.

It would make sense for me to be terrified the first time I ride my horse again. But I am not. That comes later.

When Calvin calls to say he thinks it's about time I got back in the saddle, start back with my dressage lessons, it sounds like the most reasonable proposal in the world. I had been thinking about it too, going to the stable each day, watching the girls at the barn as they take their jumping lessons on their perfectly-groomed hunters, watching Vicki take her mare Gigi around the ring in the familiar patterns of dressage. I had been trying to occupy myself by teaching Harley more stupid pet tricks on the ground, namely how to count by stamping his hoof on cue, but we had both become bored with the process and had given up. And, more and more, when I watch Calvin as he exercises Harley, I imagine myself back up there, floating in an leg yield across the diagonal of the ring, rolling with the motion of his delicate canter.

To others, my resuming riding does not appear to be, in any way, a reasonable proposal.

Mary Ellen remains silent for some minutes when I tell her of my plan: I will not attempt to ride on my own, I will always wear my helmet, I will only take lessons with Calvin in the ring, and then only for fifteen-minute intervals, but will stop at any point if the pain in my leg becomes unbearable. We are in her kitchen, my favorite part of her house. "Well," she finally says, rising to clear the dishes, "all I'm going to ask you is, really think about this."

My mother's feelings are more transparent. "If you get hurt again," she warns over the phone, "I am going to come out there and shoot that horse, then I'm going to shoot you."

"I love you too, Mom," I reply.

"My baby," she murmurs.

I schedule an extra appointment with Dr. Mesna to talk to him about this, knowing I won't receive a blessing but still wanting him to approve my course of action. I list the evidence: I don't need a crutch anymore, only the aide of a cane. I regularly go without my moon boot now. He listens, seemingly not surprised by what I am telling him. "But I won't ride if that could harm my leg," I offer.

He appears to mull this for a moment, then tells me, no, since there is a new rod in place there is little chance of it snapping. Once the bone is healed it will be much stronger than my right leg. I might experience some pain while riding because of the angle of the stirrups, but the only real concern is that blood circulation will be disturbed from the pressure, and increase swelling. "But, otherwise, since you are probably going to do it anyway," he says, "just don't fall off."

■ ■ ■

Do you know the feeling of a carousel, the wave of fancy carved horses gently moving up and down, round and around? Why should such a simple motion evoke any pleasure? But it does, and that is exactly what I feel, back up on Harley after a year. Calvin has to give me a leg up to mount from the right side; I accomplish it awkwardly, doing the motions in compete reverse from the traditional left-side mount. But I don't have any choice, the pressure on my left leg makes mounting the usual way excruciating. Calvin lengthens my stirrups so there is almost no bend in my knee, the metal of the stirrups just hitting my feet.

The movement of Harley's first steps exhilarates me, it is as if this is a brand-new sensation. Calvin leads him by the bridle, and I am a little girl on a pony ride again. But then, as if of their own accord, my hands close around the reins, my shoulders draw back to form a straight line through my hips to my heels. The body remembers.

■ ■ ■

This is why am shocked by the delayed reaction, about two weeks later, when I am in the saddle and feel real terror for the first time on horseback. It hits me like a series of slaps to the face, one stronger and more stinging than the next.

We are trotting a slow circle in the ring. Harley is going slow over the deep, even dirt, and stumbles slightly, just one step, from the sheer laziness of not picking up his front hoof. For just a moment my left leg presses against the stirrup and a jolt of pain shoots up my body, causing me to hunch over the saddle like a snail just poked with a stick. Then come the snapshots of the last year: All that blood, the morphine drip, sponge baths and the grains of canyon dirt that stubbornly clung to my scalp, X-rays of the chunk of bone missing from my leg. The days I passed alone, the clink-clink of Vicodin coming out of a bottle, and I know one thing: I never, ever want to do that again.

"Pick up a canter along the rail," Calvin says to me from the center of the ring.

I nod, gulping. *I am safe, nothing will happen.* I chant a yogi mantra, I try to remember the words to the rosary; surely syncretism is pardonable under the circumstance. I try to visualize a perfect ride, but I experience a physical rebellion. I literally can't grip the reins. A tremor runs through my body, I see it in my hands. I can't describe this feeling other than to say it seems as if I am in front of a firing squad and have heard the clicks of the hammers on the rifles being pulled back.

Worse still is that Harley realizes all this. Horses take their confidence under saddle from their rider, so when the rider is terrified the horse figures there's probably a good reason for that terror, and becomes likewise. I feel the sudden tension stiffen his back, his head flies up, his steps become mincing and tentative.

"I can't," I finally yell, near hysterical. "I'm scared, I'm so scared. Calvin!"

I don't think I have ever admitted being scared before. I brace myself for him to yell back, Get over it, just do it! This is man who jumps a horse through six-foot obstacles with a cigarette in his mouth, he is tough and rough around the edges, saving most of the gentleness within himself for horses and the barn cat.

But, instead, he slowly walks over from the center of the ring. "Whoa, laddie, whoa," he tells Harley as he takes a hold of the bridle. He reaches to put an arm around my waist and carefully guides me down. "There. That'll be enough for today." He pretends not to see the tears running from beneath my sunglasses and starts to tell me a story of a time he was sixteen. A championship show in Belfast. He'd broken his leg months before but painted the cast black like a boot and rode anyway. "I can tell you, when we came down after each jump…" he whistles slowly through his teeth. "That was something."

I nod as I listen, not knowing if this is a true story or one of his tall tales but not caring, grateful for whichever. We walk from the ring, me with my lame hobble and he trying not to seem as if he is shortening his long stride for me.

After Harley is put away and I have fed him his carrots, I feel better. Perhaps I was pressing too hard, Calvin and I agreed. The sensible thing to do is go back to basics, ride in the round pen used for training young horses. Practice the kind of exercises used to teach people to ride. You know, Calvin says, the Spanish Riding School trains their riders for years like that, it's a fine tradition. Yes, I say, that'll build confidence. Yes, we agree, that's exactly what I need to do.

■ ■ ■

My pre-op appointment comes a few days before the bone graft surgery. It is just a routine check; they want me to fill out papers saying I won't eat for 24 hours before the surgery, and have read the policies about wearing no rings, necklaces or other jewelry, come free of makeup—the one rule I always break. Really, what does a little Maybelline Great Lash hurt? I had x-rays last month, so I am not scheduled for any. Dr. Mesna, however, is the kind of careful record keeper who would rather spend the HMO's money than miss anything. He sends me to X-ray.

When the film comes back, he stands for several minutes looking at the pictures against the lighted screen in the examining room. I am lounging on the table, finishing the same *National Geographic* article I started last visit. "You guys need some new magazines," I tell him.

"Huh," he says, still looking at the film. "Huh."

"Well David?" I ask when I can stand the suspense no longer. "Anything you want to share with the class?"

I get up and stand beside him. He points to my bone. There, in the gap that has remained vacant all this time, is the fuzzy, milky image of something. From each end of the bone comes a cloudy white form that peaks, stretching out to points that touch at the tip. Michelangelo.

"Whoo-hoo!" I pat him on the arm; we are on friendly terms but hugging would be pushing it. "Houston, we have bone growth."

"Pretty good," he agrees with his usual reserve, but I can tell he's pleased. He says the fracture is healing uneventfully, meaning that nothing bad has happened. It occurs to me that medicine measures "events" in terms of the progression toward illness, disability and death, rather than measuring the increments against that progression. But today I keep my observation to myself. It's enough to see that soon I will walk on solid bone, a complete tibia that will make the titanium inside superfluous.

He cancels the surgery and sends me home with a very precise prescription: Keep doing what you're doing.

■ ■ ■

When I return to my room at Mary Ellen's I begin calling everyone in my phone book. With each I speculate on all of the possible explanations for what provoked this new bone growth: Perhaps it is simply the natural healing process, spurred by the rod replacement surgery? Or is it the yoga, lowering levels of the stress hormones in my blood stream and encouraging the formation of the calcium callus to form? I consider it all; acupuncture, tofu and meditating at five in the morning, a fat man with a beard beaming energy, sheer luck of the draw. Or, maybe, it is what Will Rogers said: Nothing is as good for the inside of a man as the outside of a horse.

When the Zen *roshi* Shunryu Suzuki was a young man he was playing the Chinese board game, Go, with a group of friends. He either was terrible at playing this strategic game, or else he was winning, because his friends suddenly turned to him and said, "Hey Suzuki, why don't you go down in the cellar and get us a watermelon? We're hungry."

So he went into the cellar, but the light was burnt out, or he forgot to turn the light on, or maybe there was no light at all and the door simply swung shut behind him cutting out the light from above, because he was wandering around in the dark, groping where he thought the melons must be. As he leaned forward pain all at once pierced his brow, a pain so nasty it took his breath away. Something warm and thick must have rolled down into his eye, and his chin and neck and chest, and he must have realized it was blood. When he tried to pull away the pain, incredibly, got meaner. Reaching up he felt for its source, discovering he was hung on a sharpened meat hook that dangled from the low ceiling. His face could have been a ham or a side of beef, it dangled just the same. He must have cried out. No one came. Tears probably rose in his eyes, running down his face, thinning the blood already there, diluting it a lighter color, which he could not see. Moving only made the hook dig in deeper, as if he were a fish caught on a line. So he could only stand there in the cool darkness, in complete stillness, not different than those melons in front of him that he could not reach. There wasn't anything to do. He breathed, his blood flowed, his heart pumped, as it does in any living mammal. When finally his friends realized that he had not brought the melon back, they came looking and found Suzuki on the hook. They must have been upset, rushing around, unsure of how to extricate him without causing more pain. When they were finished and brought him out of the cellar, they said, "Suzuki, Suzuki, what happened?" And he said, "I was awakened."

That plan Calvin and I hatched about me riding in the round pen, like the riders of Austria's famed Spanish Riding School, that was a good plan.

Because, really, who would believe anything could happen when, on a warm Saturday afternoon a couple of months later, Harley is trotting calmly in the small pen, me sitting in the saddle without my stirrups to practice balance and ease the pressure off my bad leg? Doing the same old thing we know by rote now?

What are the odds? A long shot, for sure—that a child, perhaps four or five years old, who has never been to any barn before, is brought to this stable by her parents, friends of someone just passing through? And, further, that this child, unfamiliar with barn rules—how could she know there were rules?—should be left unattended by these parents, who are so very glad to see their friend, gosh it's been such a long time? And no one would guess that this child should decide it would be fun to play pop-goes-the-weasel, with herself as the weasel, as the lady on the brown horsy go by.

Who would even speculate that a child would hide on the lower railing and spring up to the side of the pen just as the brown horsy and the lady pass?

No one would see it coming when such an act as a playful child popping up would startle the brown horsy just slightly and causes him to make a quick step to the side, as if to avoid the child, should she land in his way?

And that, meanwhile, this popping girl *See her brown hair* would distract the lady for just a second, but it is that very same second in which her brown horsy steps to the side? And that this slight loss of balance would be enough to slip the lady from the saddle, so that she tumbles—almost in slow motion, everyone will note later—to the deep, sandy ground?

This fall would not be serious, like tipping from a barstool to land on a firm mattress. Except that—and here's the real believe-it-or-not—the horsy halts as the lady spills from his back to the ground. It would be likely that the horsy then would just move forward, out of the way of his fallen rider. But because of the angle of the round pen, the horsy can't move forward, so he takes one step backwards. And in making this step backward, the horsy's hind hoof hits the scared tissue of the lady's titanium leg, where the bone is still not united, where more than 50 percent of the blood supply has already been destroyed.

■ ■ ■

My nightmare real, again. *And when I am pinned.*

■ ■ ■

Harley's soft nose is in my face, his ears up, as if to say, What are you doing down there again? Calvin is right beside me. "Can you stand, luv? Are you hit?"

I grab onto his arm. *I don't want to look I don't want to look.* But I do, and there I am, amazingly, in one piece. The anklebone connected to the shin bone, the shin bone connected to the knee bone. Just like the song. The thick leather of my chaps running uninterrupted on both sides.

"Can you stand?" says Calvin in the tone he usually saves for skittish colts. I say I think so. Sore, but yes, I can. He pulls me up. "There, that a girl," he says.

And then there I am, on two feet, not bleeding.

What had seemed to hang as a moment suspended now breaks into fast forward. Calvin bellows, "What idjut is responsible for this? She could have been killed!" His face is very red, he looks very close to hitting something. Drew is yelling something too, the little girl starts to cry, Janice says "I'll get some ice, Sam, come sit down," Juan moves quickly into the pen to grab Harley's reins.

"Momento, por favor," I ask him. My voice shaky, feeling weak in the knees. I lean into Harley and hug his neck. "It's OK," I tell my brown horse, "It's not like before." I look at Juan. "I don't want him to be scared," I say.

Juan nods. "Si. Yo sey."

I arrange myself on the lawn chair Janice hastily prepares, elevate and ice-pack my leg and take the four Motrin Janice supplies to keep the swelling down. Drew brings my cell phone, "Call your doctor, just to be safe." He's right. I leave a message that begins, "I'm fine, but…"

The mother of the child brings her up to me to apologize. The girl's copper eyes are huge with fear and incomprehension, unsure still of the cause that created this explosive effect. "I'm fine honey," I say to her softly, like telling a secret her mom can't hear, "but you and I just have to learn to be very, very aware around horses. They're so big!"

She nods, then tucks her chin tight, not looking at me.

I reach a hand to touch her tiny arm. "That way we don't get into accidents. OK?"

The girl turns her big eyes to me once more. I think, should I tell her horses are dangerous? Will fear teach her anything that will save her from scars and pain and confusion? Will it prevent her heart from breaking, ever?

Or will my words become one of the bricks in a wall she will eventually come to live inside? Will it make her recede into a careful world where even the mildest discomfort is avoided, a life in bubble wrap? Thirty years from now, will she be the kind of woman who always turns away from, rather than into, all the not-for-sures, all the no-guarantees?

I would rather see her scarred and limping.

In this moment I see clearly the point to which that

canyon trail led. I will no longer run away from my life, careering and oblivious, equally blind to what is in front of me as I am to what is behind. I will run into my life, with my eyes wide open and my hands outstretched. I will know as best I am able the singular texture of each moment. There is no other destination.

EPILOGUE.

There is a tiny guest house painted white, a cottage more like, at the end of a road about five miles up a canyon in Malibu. The house is on the down slope of a hillside covered in twisting, purple-flowered vines of vinca. It is the same canyon to which I first moved four years ago when I was married. There is a steep flight of stairs that leads from the road down to a deck, and to the front door. I always make sure to hold the railing going up and down. I move slowly still, but, some days, it doesn't hurt at all. Some days, I don't even limp.

On the deck I have potted trees and an asparagus fern that keeps trying to die on me. There is a table covered with a bright mint-checked tablecloth, I put it in the corner by the railing. That's where all my friends like to sit and take in the view of the mountains when they come to visit. Sometimes we have to duck and cover when the crazy flock of escaped green parrots flies over, they squawk and haggle with each other like street merchants. Edward says they have been up in these parts for years.

There is also a fleece-lined dog bed for Ming. Her age has finally caught up to her; she sleeps more than ever now, when not being hassled and annoyed by Goshi, the Akita puppy Gurmukh gave me as a birthday gift. He weights about eighty pounds now, and is supposed to sleep in a large crate that is also on the deck. But most nights and all day he sleeps on my bed. I have lots of bookshelves, which is wonderful, and a glass-top desk Renee gave me. The dust that keeps collecting there is a constant reminder I'm still not a good housekeeper.

In the kitchen, my shelves are stocked full of food my mother insists on sending in her regular care packages from New Mexico. The refrigerator is covered in the cut-out comics she always includes.

By the handle of the freezer hangs my first and only blue ribbon, "First Place Pomona Chapter Schooling Show." It's kind of silly, really; there were only about five riders in the show, held in someone's backyard arena, so we were all guaranteed a first place in something. I couldn't fit into a pair of real hunt boots that day, because my leg is a little hard to fit—I keep saying when my ship comes in I'll splurge for a pair of custom-made. It didn't matter what I wore, at any rate. Harley walked, trotted and cantered on cue. I was worried I would confuse the points where we were supposed to turn or circle, but, in the end, I paid attention and remembered everything just fine. As we rode up the centerline of the arena toward the judge, Calvin was hooting and hollering and carrying on like we had just won a gold medal.

Only a few of my friends have seen my little ribbon hanging on the refrigerator. But that's OK. I know it's there.

Each afternoon at about three I quit whatever I'm doing and head down the hill to the stable. Those paddock boots that were new three years ago now have cracks in the leather, and I think I'll need to get them re-soled before long. Harley and I just ride around in the ring, although he always looks up toward to the area where the trail comes down, ears pricked tightly forward. It's probably just because of the construction noise; they're building a bunch of new homes up there now. Still, sometimes I wonder what he sees. What he remembers.

The other day I didn't ride 'til late again, and a thick blanket of fog was just rolling in off the Pacific. The fog grew denser still as we rode, blurring the shapes of things with its opal dust. As we cantered along the rail a gust blew toward us and we were enveloped for an instant. The ground disappeared, and all I felt were four good legs beneath me, going forward. Where, I could not see.

ACKNOWLEDGEMENTS

Many years now have passed since that blood-filled day in the canyon. Lingering pain in my leg fluctuates from bad to worse, but most days I try to let this pain serve to remind me to be grateful for the life I have—which, I have to tell you, is pretty damn great.

I forever want to extend my appreciation and respect to Matt, who endured painful and difficult times with me. He has been married to an amazing, generous woman for many years now, and is the father of two beautiful daughters.

If wealth were measured in friendships, I would be a billionaire. Loving friends who also happen to be deep thinkers and talented writers enrich my existence in ways I find it hard to express. I'm afraid I've impinged upon their generous natures more than once—raided their refrigerators, drank their wine, and plucked their brains. I could not have finished *Not By Accident* without support from: Mary Rakow and Lola Wiloughby, Janet Fitch, Mary Ellen Strote, Renée Vogel, Beverly Olevin, Cassandra Clark, and the incomparable Sandra Tsing Loh. I would not have put it back into print without encouragement from the likes of Jamie Rose, Amanda Fletcher, David Ulin, and especially Deanne Stillman.

I want to thank my oldest, best friend, Tina Griego. For what? Everything. Years ago, Gurmukh Kaur Khalsa, Father Mike Heher, and William *Yoshin* Jodran *Sensei* taught me what it means to walk a path. I still try in my imperfect way to live up to their example.

The publishing world can be hard, but within it there are many allies for writers: Alex Siegel Postman first encouraged me to take notes, and to write about my accident. Übermensches Peter Matson and Jim Rutman at Sterling Lord Literistic started me on this journey, and now I continue it with the feisty and sharp Lynn Johnston. I'm grateful to Brooke Warner and the team at She Writes Press for their commitment to reissuing this work.

Many books and articles informed and influenced my thinking during the course of writing, among them *Shifting the Blame: Literature, Law, and the Theory of Accidents in Nineteenth-Century America*, by Nan Goodman; *Target Risk*, by Gerald J.S. Wilde, PhD; *Why We Hurt: The Natural History of Pain*, by Dr. Frank T. Vertosick, Jr.; and the essay "Purebreds and Amazons: Saying Things With Horses in Late-Nineteenth-Century France," by Kari Weil.

I will also always be indebted to the emergency team at UCLA Hospital, and to Dr. David Mesna and the orthopedic staff at Kaiser Permanente Hospital, Woodland Hills, California, for their top-rate care. Acupuncturist Steve Lee's healing hands helped put me together, body and mind. Dr. Jared Strote, you write great e-mails. Thank you for being my resident expert. Thanks to everyone at Malibu Vista Ranch for caring for Harley when I couldn't.

But this full, wonderful life of mine has not been not without sadness in these years.

If Edward Albert Jr. had not saved my life, I would not be typing these words right now. He and his wife, Kate Woodville, and daughter, Tai Carmen, became true family to me. Now both Kate and Edward have passed, but I am grateful to say that Tai and I still call each other "sister."

Also lost to me is my friend the writer and teacher Les Plesko, who ended his own life in 2013. His keen eye sharpened my work and his humor and soul sweetened everything.

I still miss my complicated grandmother, Evelyn, who taught me to look for the meanings of things. But perhaps the hardest loss has been that of my mom, Deanne Harris. Mom, please hear this from wherever you are: I am proud to be your daughter.

As I chronicle in another book, Harley died suddenly, in his early twenties, on a sad winter night. I was lucky to have Edward, Kate, and my mom there with me at the time, before they too left too early to go into the great unknown forever.

In the wake of pain and loss it is hard to imagine happiness and fulfillment could be waiting out there. Yet it was. A man named Jimmy Camp and I have built a life and a future together. Our son, Benen, arrived unplanned and unexpectedly in 2009. The meaning of his name is the final word I'll give you: blessed.

SAMANTHA DUNN
2015

ABOUT THE AUTHOR

PHOTO CREDIT: MARGOT ROSE

SAMANTHA DUNN is the author of *Failing Paris*, a finalist for the PEN West Fiction Award in 2000, and the memoir *Faith in Carlos Gomez: A Memoir of Salsa, Sex and Salvation*. Her essays have appeared in numerous national publications, including the *Los Angeles Times*, *O Magazine*, *Ms.*, and *Salon*. She teaches at the Idyllwild Arts Center and in the UCLA Extension Writers Program, where she was named 2011 Instructor of the Year. Dunn lives in Orange, California.

SELECTED TITLES FROM SHE WRITES PRESS

She Writes Press is an independent publishing company
founded to serve women writers everywhere. Visit us at
www.shewritespress.com.

Four Funerals and a Wedding: Resilience in a Time of Grief by
Jill Smolowe. $16.95, 978-1-938314-72-8. When journalist
Jill Smolowe lost four family members in less than two years,
she turned to modern bereavement research for answers—and
made some surprising discoveries.

A Leg to Stand On: An Amputee's Walk into Motherhood by Colleen
Haggerty. $16.95, 978-1-63152-923-8. Haggerty's candid story
of how she overcame the pain of losing a leg at seventeen—and
of terminating two pregnancies as a young woman—and went
on to become a mother, despite her fears.

Renewable: One Woman's Search for Simplicity, Faithfulness, and Hope
by Eileen Flanagan. $16.95, 978-1-63152-968-9. At age forty-nine,
Eileen Flanagan had an aching feeling that she wasn't living up to
her youthful ideals or potential, so she started trying to change the
world—and in doing so, she found the courage to change her life.

Where Have I Been All My Life? A Journey Toward Love and Wholeness
by Cheryl Rice. $16.95, 978-1-63152-917-7. Rice's universally
relatable story of how her mother's sudden death launched her on
a journey into the deepest parts of grief—and, ultimately, toward
love and wholeness.

Splitting the Difference: A Heart-Shaped Memoir by Tré Miller-
Rodríguez. $19.95, 978-1-938314-20-9. When 34-year-old
Tré Miller-Rodríguez's husband dies suddenly from a heart attack,
her grief sends her on an unexpected journey that culminates in
a reunion with the biological daughter she gave up at 18.

Fire Season: A Memoir by Hollye Dexter. $16.95, 978-1-63152-974-0.
After she loses everything in a fire, Hollye Dexter's life spirals
downward and she begins to unravel—but when she finds herself
at the brink of losing her husband, she is forced to dig within
herself for the strength to keep her family together.

CPSIA information can be obtained at www.ICGtesting.com
Printed in the USA
BVOW03s0924230615

405749BV00001B/1/P